Contemporary African Art Abstracted

by

Valentine
MUTASA

Environmental Distress — CLIMATE CHANGE
Our mothers — My sisters
My Visions in Abstract Terms

ARTWORKS

Curated

By

Alf Muronda MFA

Acknowledgements

Thank you to Valentine's mother, Faina Maenzanise, without whose inspiration, assistance, and critical eye, it would have been near impossible for Valentine to complete the critical artworks included in the Environmental Distress, Climate Change and Our Mothers, My Sisters' portfolios.

Much gratitude to Raphael Chikukwa, the Executive Director of the Zimbabwe National Gallery whose review and comments in the first iteration of this book helped me improve the presentation of Valentine's artworks in this version of the book..

Thank you to Chelsea and Annah, Valentine's sister and wife for your assistance and patience with Valentine and I in getting this work done.

PERSONAL PHOTOGRAPHY: Tambudzai Bridgette Kambani

ARTWORKS PHOTOGRAPHY: Muronda Studio Graphics

Please Note:

- Except were indicated, all artworks are oil on canvass.

- The pictorial presentation of the artworks is for representation and information purposes only. Where possible the actual size of the artwork is listed with the artwork.

ISBN 978-1-965398-22-7

© Valentine K Mutasa/E.F.Muronda

Published By: MASAKA PUBLISHING MEDIA HOUSE
Harare, Zimbabwe—Cherry Hill, New Jersey
alf@cp7sisters.com

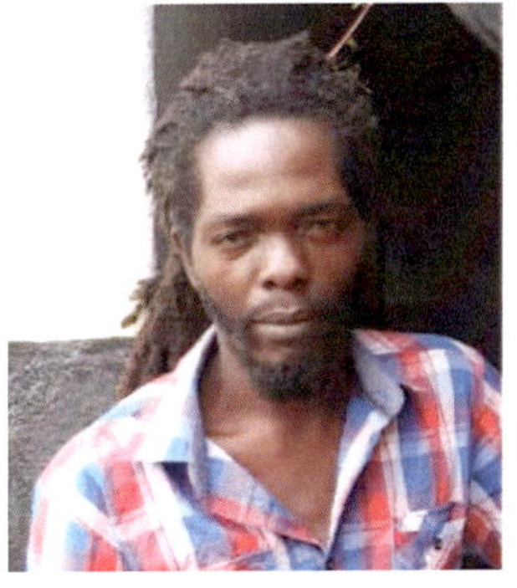

Valentine Kumbirai Mutasa

Valentine Kumbirai Mutasa, uses his artistic paint brush as a social commentary on existential issues that affect us all. His work is reflective and instructive of the issues that are close to is heart, the degradation of his environment because of natural and man made disasters and the complex role of women as mother and sister in his life reflecting their lives both as victims and triumphant survivors who remain strong and beautiful bringing forth life.

At 43, Valentine, who was born and grew up in Mbare township in the shadow of the City of Harare, is an iconic symbol of his African township roots, where he is known as an artist-warrior whose studio is the open backyard of his humble home.

In his neighborhood where he was nicknamed "Picasso" from a very young age, Valentine is known as a creative force that brings both young and old members of the community together. His open air artist studio, which is no more than the walls of his family home, behind the semi-detached matchbox houses that characterize his neighborhood, is a place where community members, young and old, gather for boisterous banter and commiseration. In the process of discussion and debates, with a paintbrush in one hand and a finger remonstrating in the air to make a point in the other, Valentine holds court encouraging the young and decrying the abject poverty that surrounds him and the attendant socials ills that come with it.

The artworks presented herein ranging from environmental destruction, climate change distress, women as mothers and sisters and general portraiture in abstracts were done by Valentine in his backyard whenever the weather permitted because on rainy days and the biting chilly days of winter, the studio is closed.

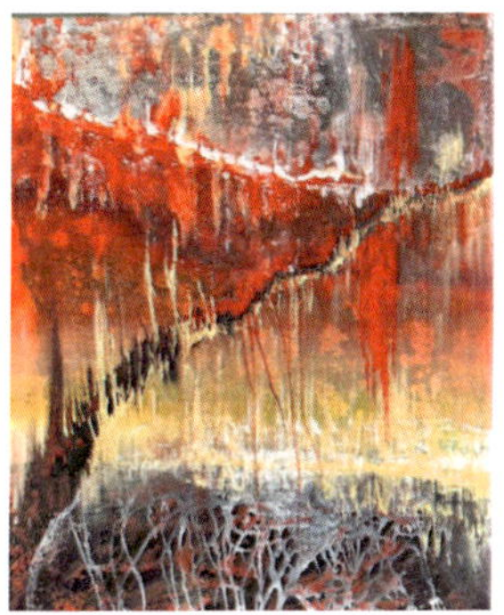

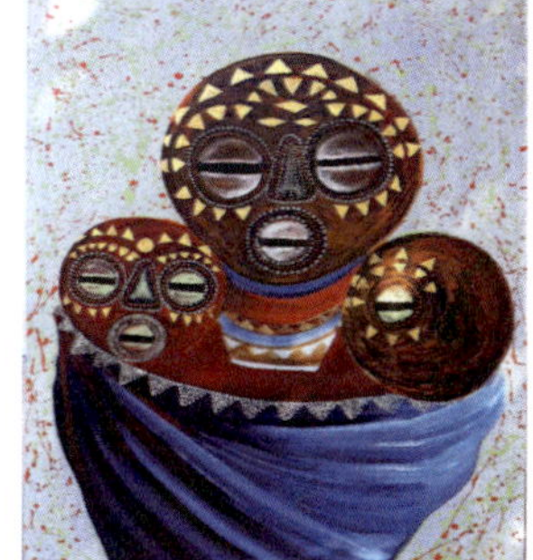

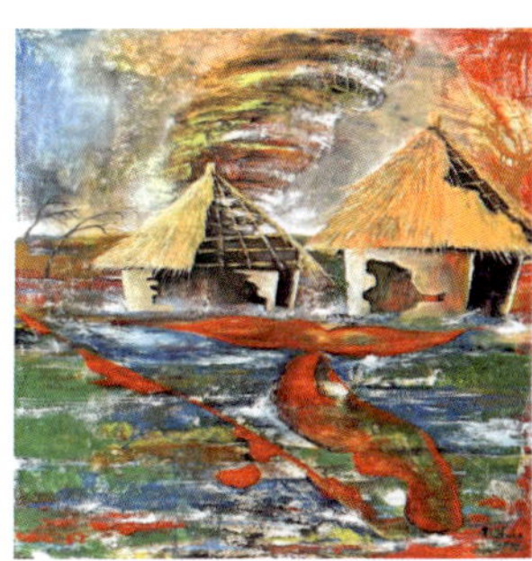

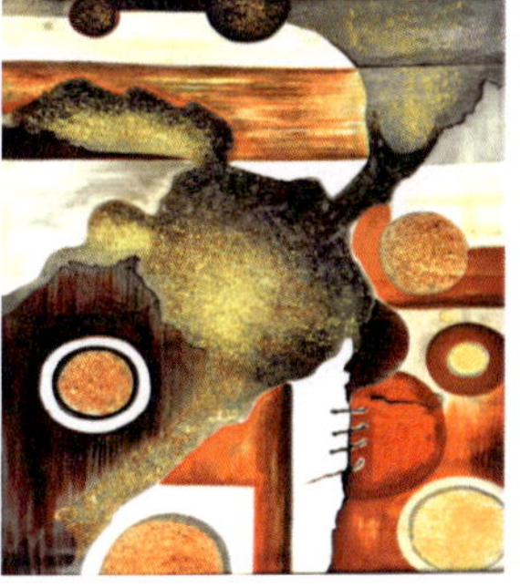

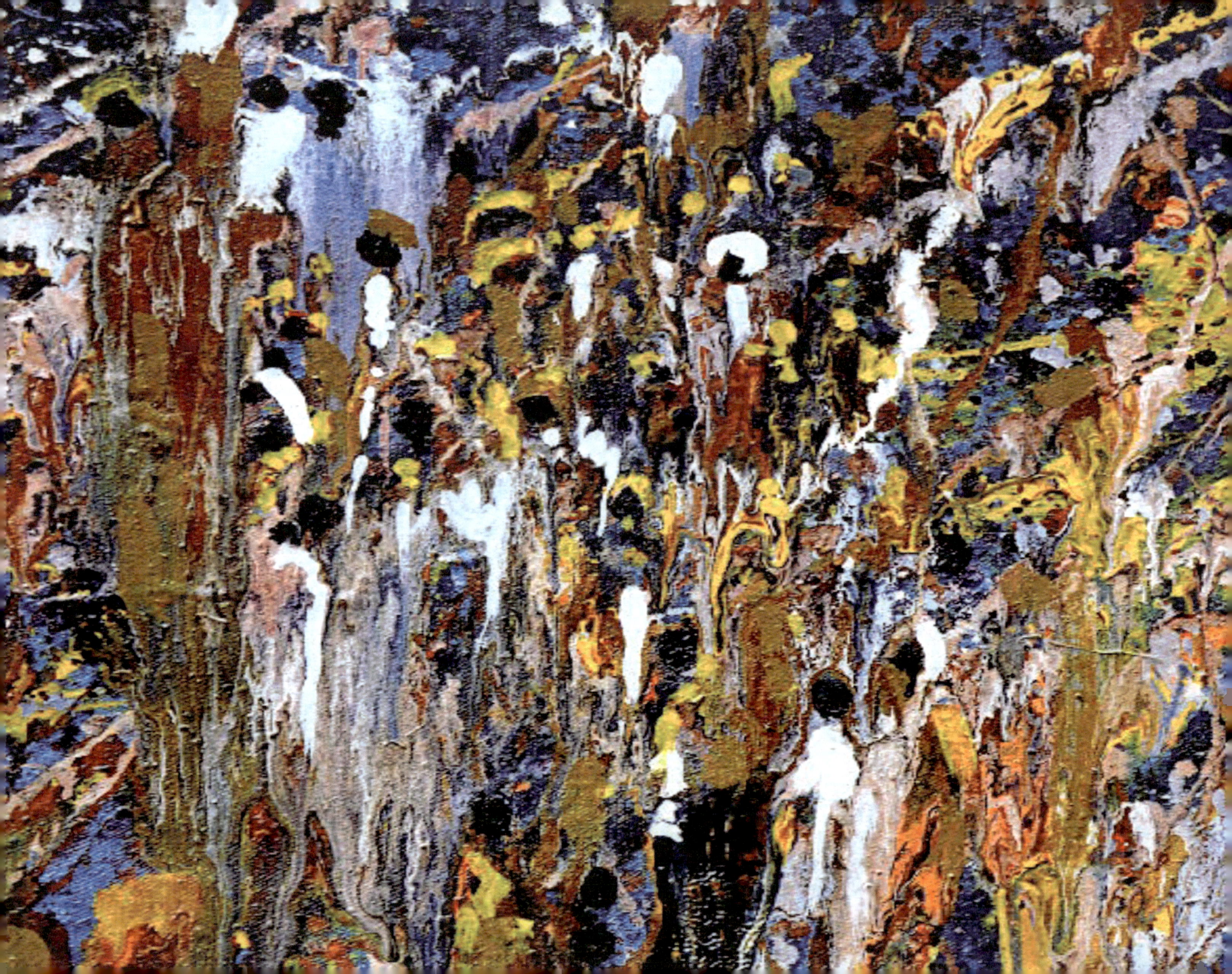

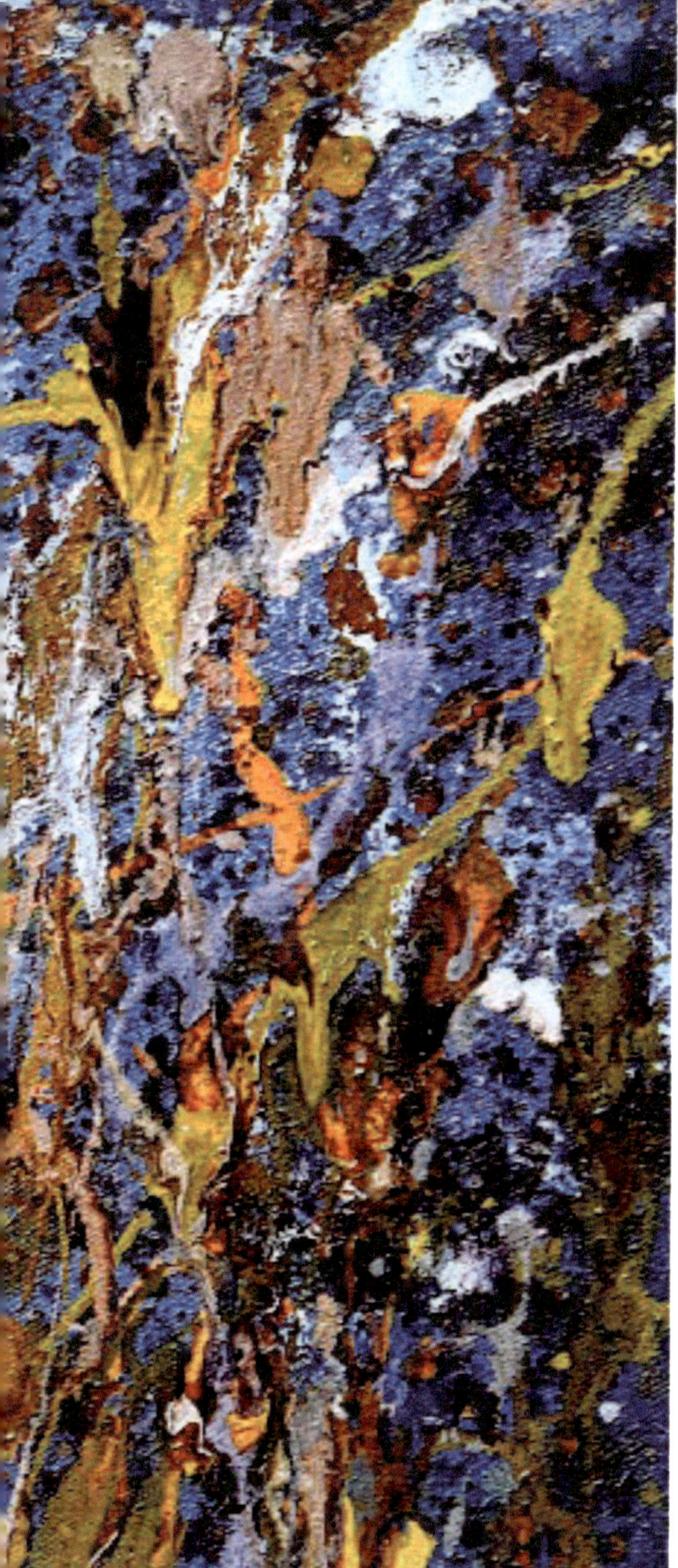

How I met Valentine
By Alf Muronda

I have always loved art in its various forms for as long as I can remember. I grew up in the townships of Harare as a photographer's son. At a very young age, in his studio in Matapi Hostels, my father introduced me to art by letting me help him to colorize black & white portrait photographs for his clients. Taking after my father, I eventually trained and graduated from UCLA's Master of Fine Arts program. Besides photography and film, I write and paint though I would not call myself an artist like Valentine.

Sometime in 2004 on a typical tropical sunny weekday in Harare, I was walking in the business district of Zimbabwe's capital city when I came across a street vendor selling sheets of some kind of art on canvas. What caught my eye was the mélange of bright red paint and other earth tone colors that served as a background to stick figures drawn to depict African men and women in various poses.

The splashes of black ink on those canvasses depicting images of African people that was passing for art annoyed me greatly to say the least. I was so personally offended that my first instinct was to buy the whole lot and dump it somewhere where no one would ever see such abomination. The art the vendor was selling consisted of uncomplimentary stick figures of Africans featuring exaggerated lips, exaggerated hips, skinny legs, with oblong black heads, the perfect picture of a buffoon. As much as I was offended, I was also fascinated by the palette of colors set in a visual harmony that made the very same obnoxious canvasses so attractive.

(continued overleaf)

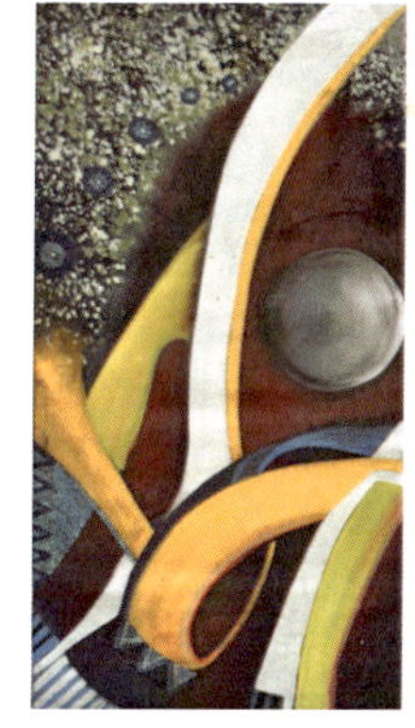

There was a scribbled signature on some, but it was unreadable. I asked the vendor who the artist was and where he got his merchandise from. The vendor had no interest in answering any questions except to ask if I was buying or not. I think because of my familiarity and language the vendor saw me more as competition than the typical tourist the vendors catered for.

So, he would not tell me. I left him without buying and resumed my walk. Then on the next street around the corner in the tourist hub in the shadow of the 5-star Meikles Hotel, I ran into more vendors all selling the same "artworks". Today, just as then, I am not sure what was driving me to want to find

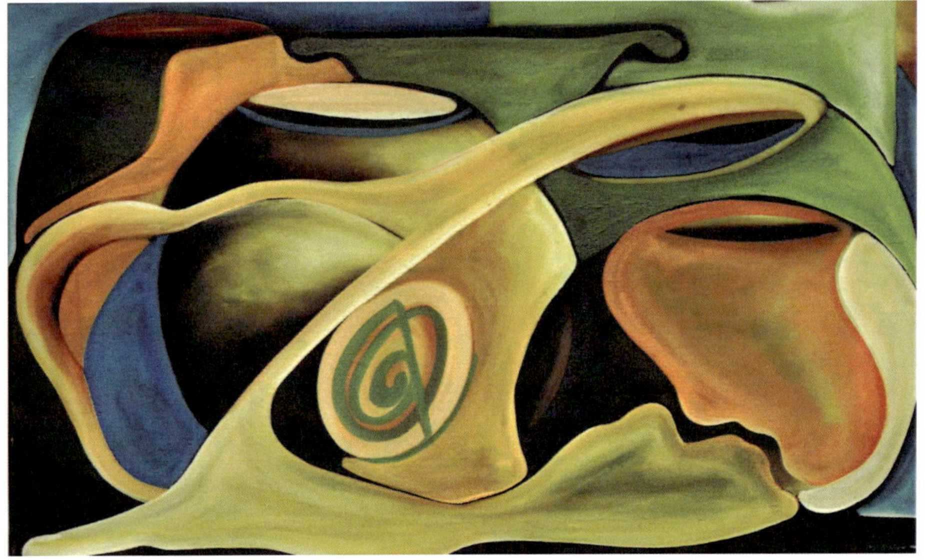

the source of these canvasses, but I was drawn in all the way. I forgot about the trip to wherever it was that I was supposed to be going to and decided that I was I going to find the source of these canvasses. After many inquiries, I eventually struck a deal with one of the vendors who broke ranks with the other vendors. I assured him that I was not trying to compete with them or cut them out from what apparently was the good business deal they had going selling these canvasses. The deal was I would buy the six canvasses he had left in stock because he was closing shop for the day and pay him to take me to the source of his merchandize. With the vendor as my guide, I drove to Mbare the township I grew up in and ended up in a section

known as KwaMarova. I pulled up to one of the nondescript semidetached houses in a long block on one of the narrow-tarred roads near the hostels, a road with hardly any traffic passing by. In the yard of the house and on the road in front of the house, I found myself looking at a group of boisterous boys and young men any one of whom could have been myself at an earlier age. There must have been at least 15 of them, their ages, I guess, ranged from about 12 to 20 years old. A few were milling about, cracking jokes, smoking cigarettes, but most of them were organized in an assembly line. They were painting the obnoxious canvasses by committee.

The canvasses were lined up laid on the edge of the tarred road. With buckets of black paint in tow, some of the boys were assigned to painting the heads while others were painting the torsos in the designated places and others painted in the skinny legs etc, etc. The efficiency of the whole operation explained why they were so many of these canvasses floating around. So here I was at the source of the artwork that had rankled me and all I could do was shake my head and laugh at myself. There was no "artist" to attribute the canvasses to, it was just a well-organized enterprise by unemployed youth from the neighborhood that I had grown up in. Though their product was an artistic abomination in my view, I was impressed by the ingenuity of their commercial (continued on p71)

Environmental Distress

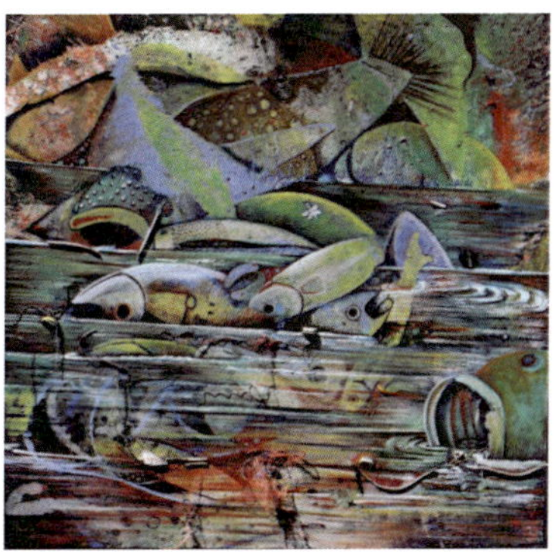

Valentine's artworks tell the story of the environmental distress in his world. Besides the vagaries of climate change, he decries unregulated mining activities that have damaged the landscape in rural communities and pollution from industrial factory waste dumped into the local rivers that surround his township home. On canvas, Valentine captures the ecological consequences of that horrendous assault on nature in pursuit of profit and our comfort.

- Except were indicated, all artworks are oil on canvass. The pictorial presentation of the artworks is for representation and information purposes only. Where possible the actual size of the art-work is listed with the artwork.

The New Tree of Life

The New Tree of Life painting is a symbolic construct of the contradiction between human achievement in invention in industry and technology juxtaposed with the destructive byproducts of the same achievements. The painting is a metaphorical statement representing the futility of mankind's technical and industrial pyrrhic achievements because the same achievements have not only severely compromised the planet's natural ecological systems, but have also initiated the unprecedented causes of global warming resulting in a change in the climate which, if unabated, could easily result in the extermination and extinction of both the wildlife and mankind itself on Planet Earth, in the way of the dinosaurs.

The painting is a mixed media artwork centered around a tree made of discarded electrical wire as its tree trunk and branches, with junky plastic knickknacks of manufactured byproducts like toothbrushes, bottle caps etc. for its leaves, planted on a slice of the earth whose mineral wealth, which lie below the surface under the tree roots, is symbolized by an encrusted salve made of a muted crystalized mixture of finely ground glass, dirt and tiny, tiny stones. I happened to be visiting the day he finished this masterpiece. It was an amazing

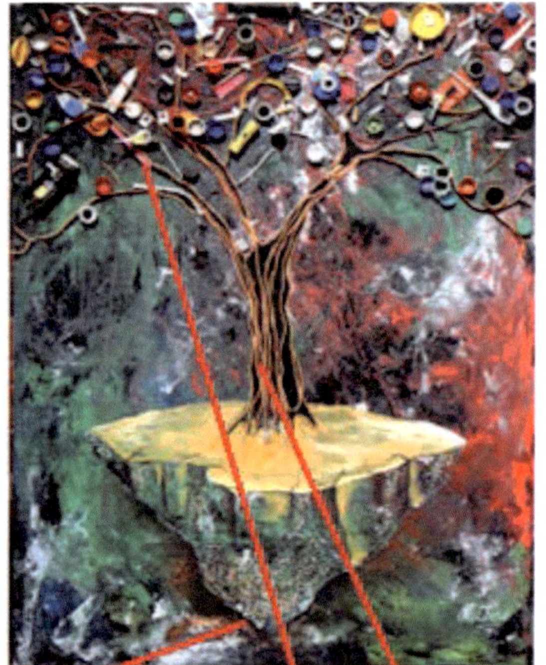

experience watching to see Valentine's creative mind and his fingers at work. When it was finished, I asked him what it meant and how he had come up with this incredible piece of interpretive artwork.   Valentine said: *"...the inspiration came to me after I had passed by a mining area somewhere in the reserves not too far from here where people were mining gold or whatever. When I came back something struck me about the scenes I had witnessed. People were extracting gold and other minerals from mines, from the land and leaving trees and the natural vegetation dying. There was no one and nothing to replace the trees or anything to make that land fertile again. So I started thinking, they are mining and destroying earth for industrial use or for money. They make their money from the natural resources of the earth and they thank that same earth by producing plastic bags and other plastic products and other things that cannot be recycled. So instead of leaves from trees falling to the ground and fertilizing it, their manmade products litter the earth and get buried where no vegetation can ever grow again. The senselessness of it all just puzzled me. That's how this painting has come about."*

His explanation was so simple and yet so profound, it said it all.

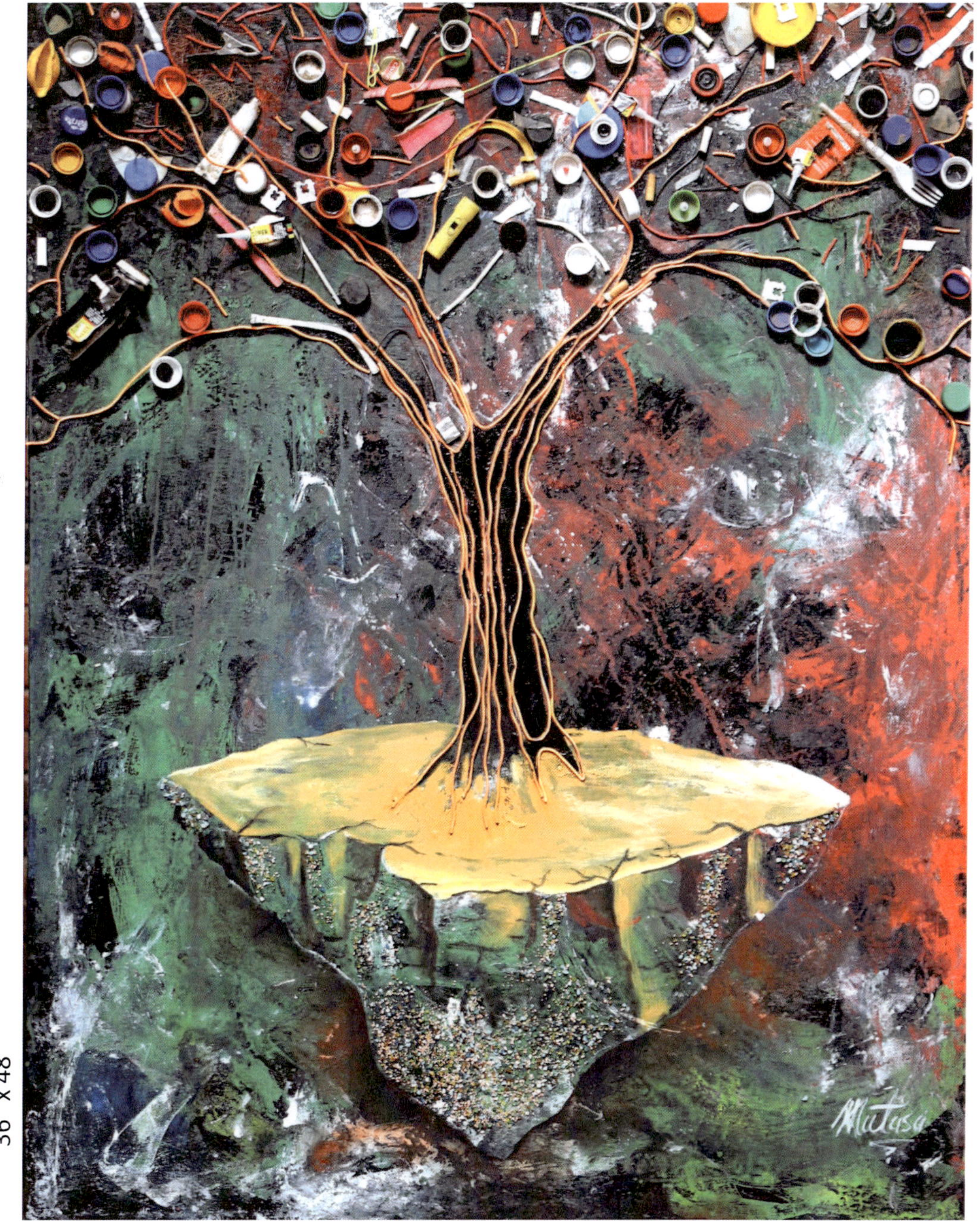

36" x 48"

The New Tree of Life   V2023   Mixed Media   91 x 123cm

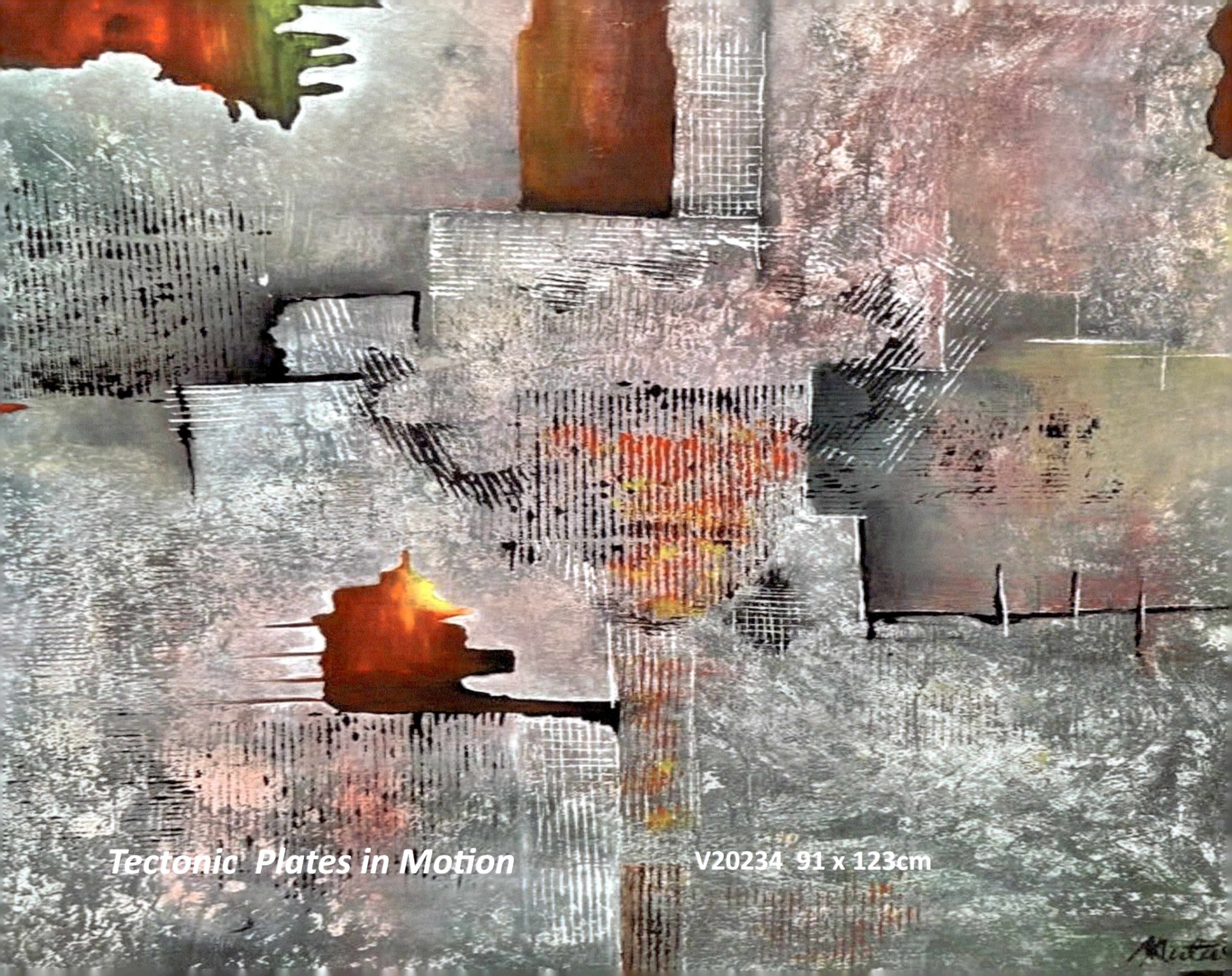

Tectonic Plates in Motion
V20234 91 x 123cm

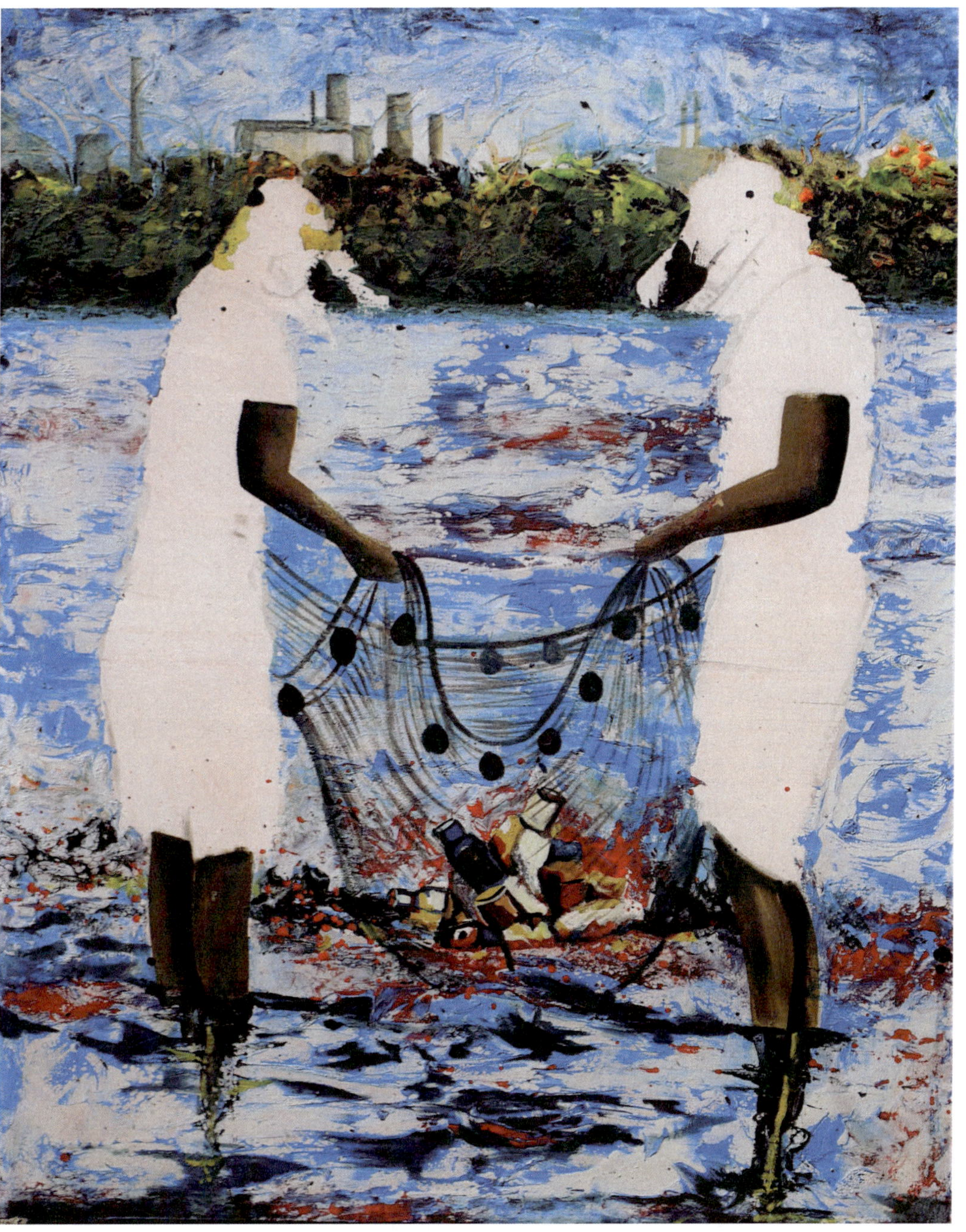

Today's Catch V20232 Oil on Canvas 91 x 123cm

36" x 48"

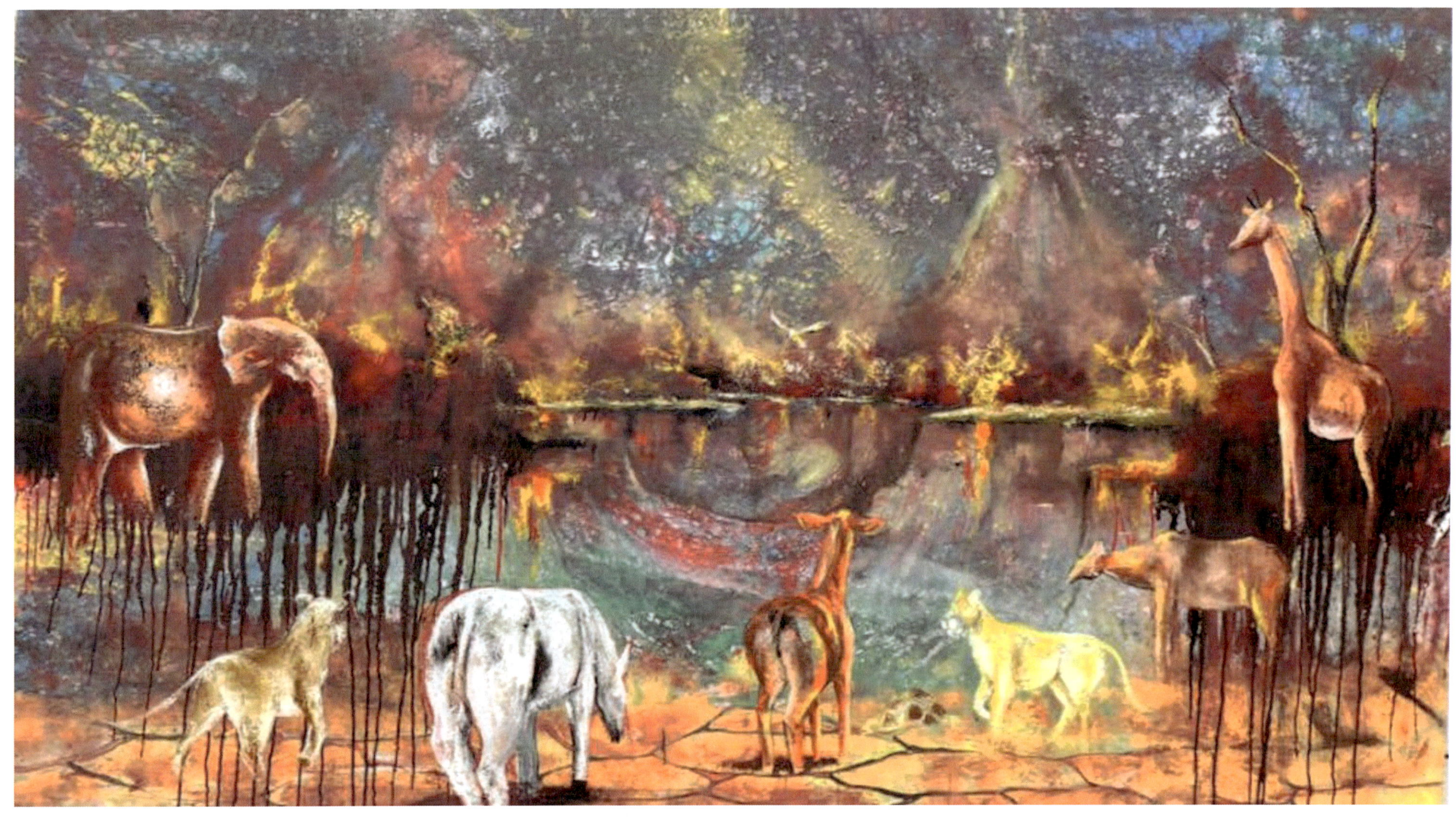

Polluted Spring　　　　　　V20233　　　　　　152 x 91 cm   (60" x 36")

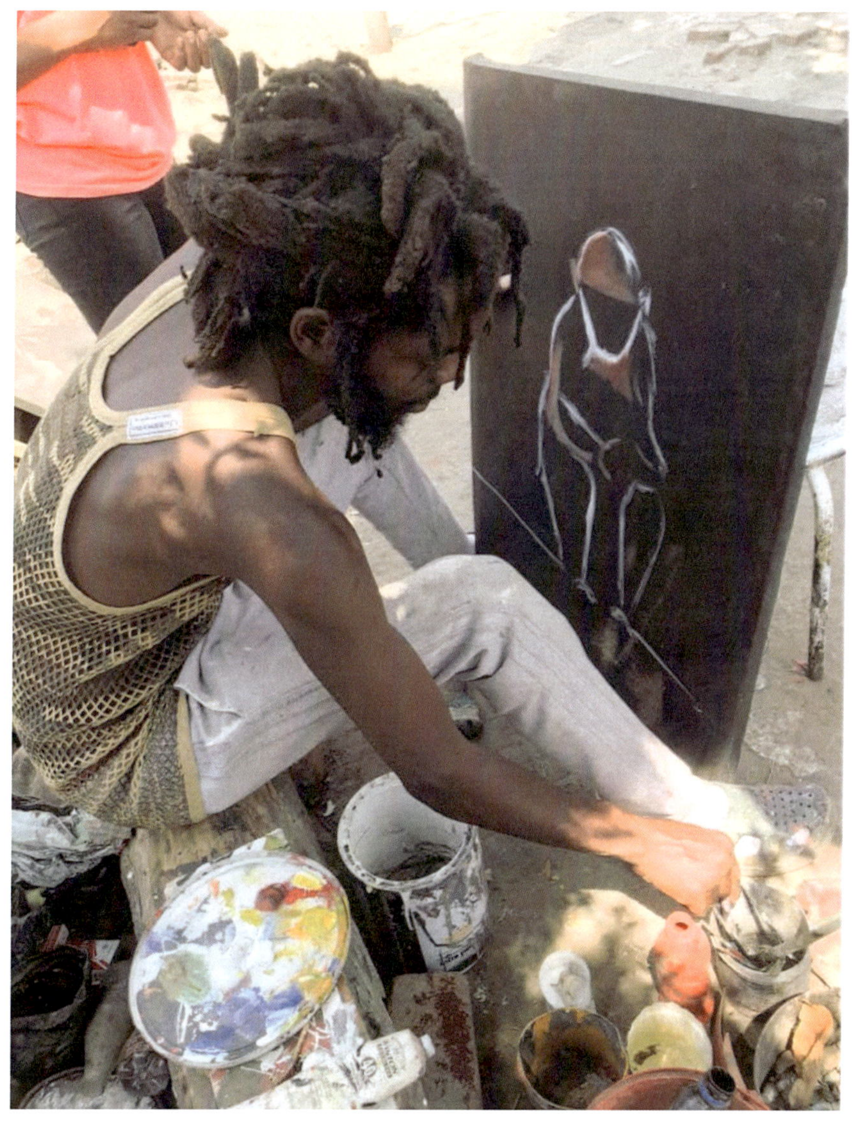

Valentine

in

his

studio

in

the

backyard.

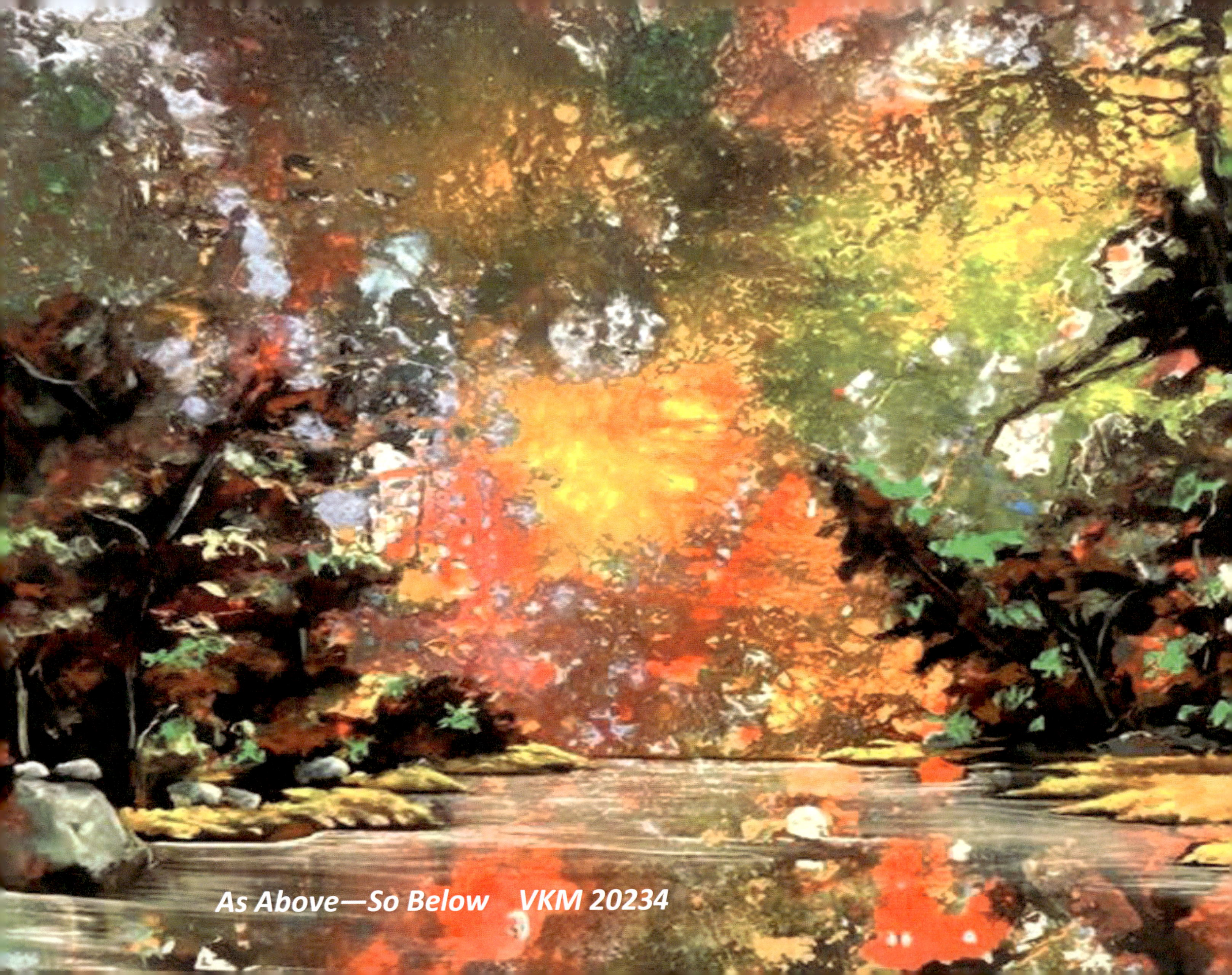
As Above—So Below   VKM 20234

Our Mothers

My Sisters

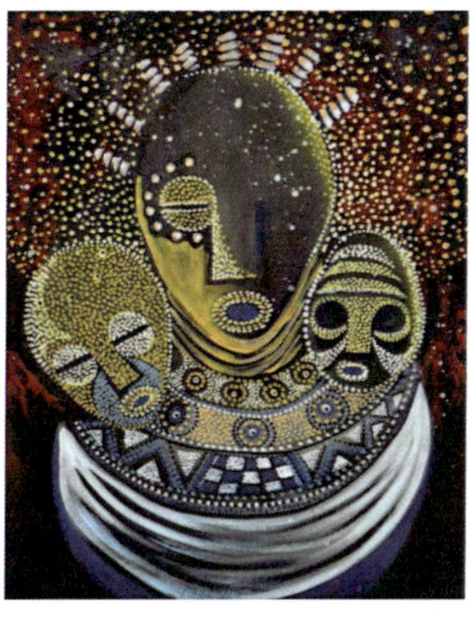

Growing up in a single-mother-headed household has had a profound influence on Valentine's perspective on the women in his life.

His paintings of women evoke both the strength of their spirit as well as their vulnerability.

He paints the women not only as the earth-keepers, child educators and child protectors but also as market women who do whatever they have to do to make a living.

His female figures can be full bodied confident women bathing at the river or the hapless somber young single mother whose prospects in life do not seem so promising.

- Except were indicated, all artworks are oil on canvass. The pictorial presentation of the artworks is for representation and information purposes only. Where possible the actual size of the artwork is listed with the artwork.

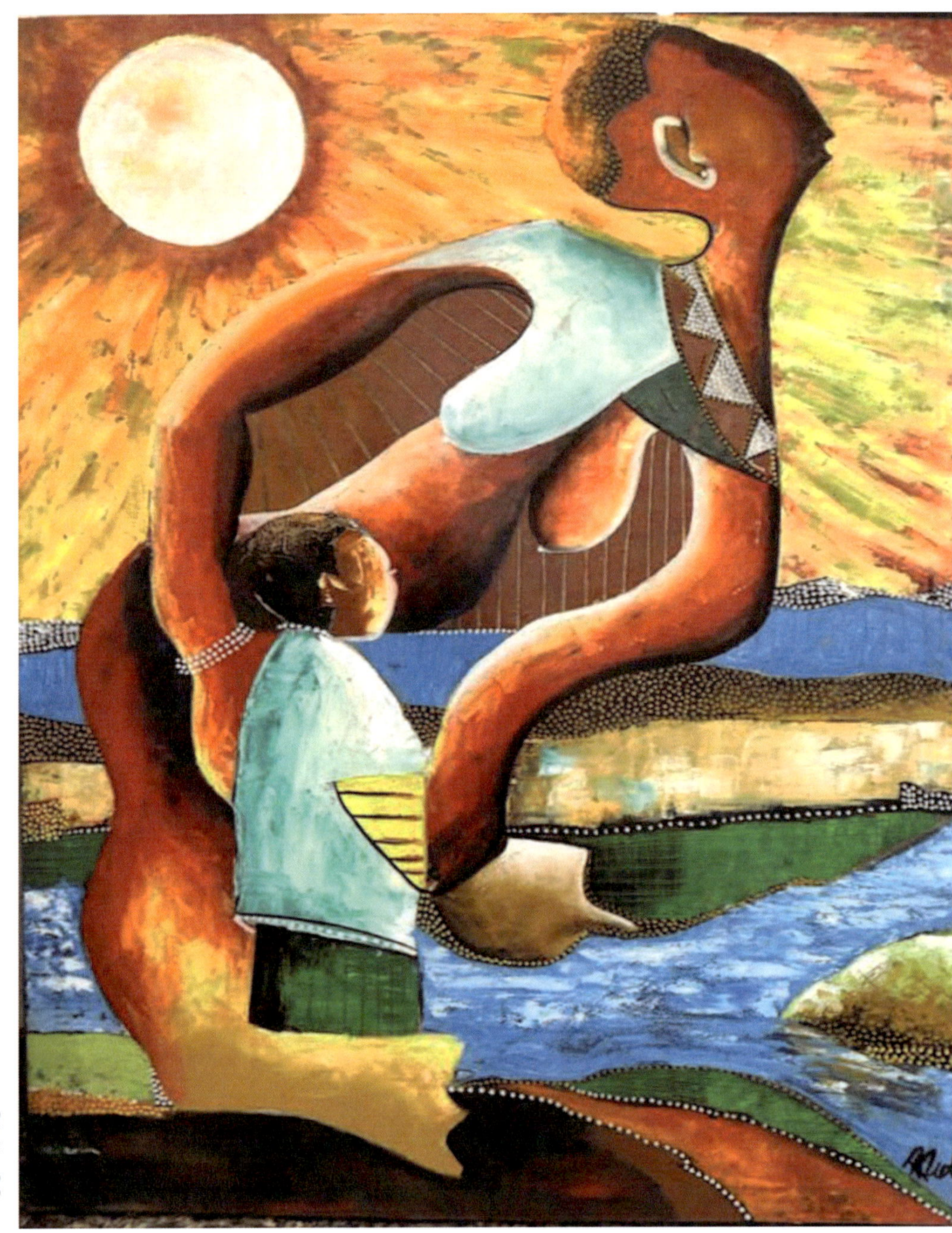

V20235
91 x 123cm

36" x 48"

Earth Mother Warrior Spirit #1

V20236
91 x 123cm

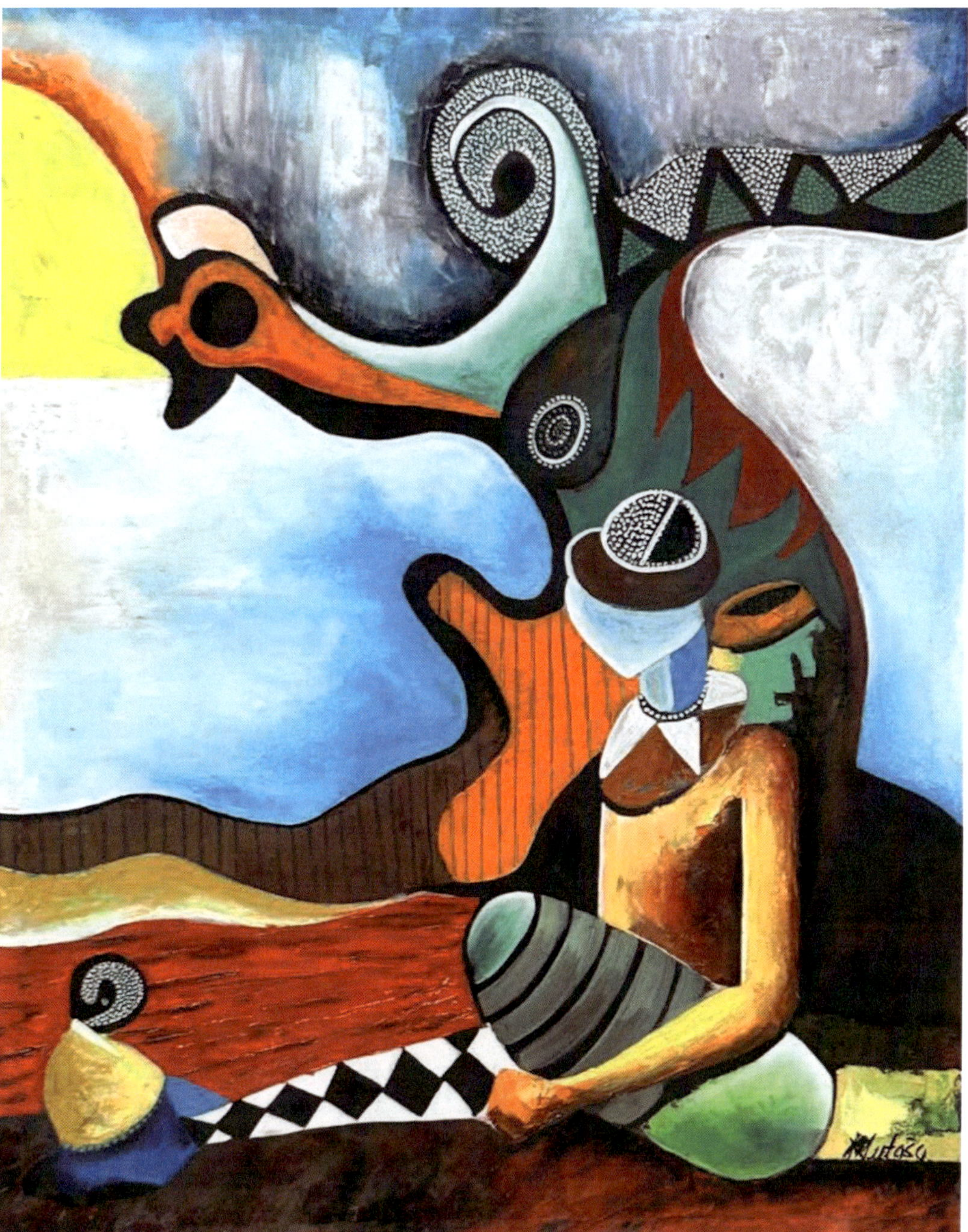

36" x 48"

Earth Mother Warrior Spirit #2

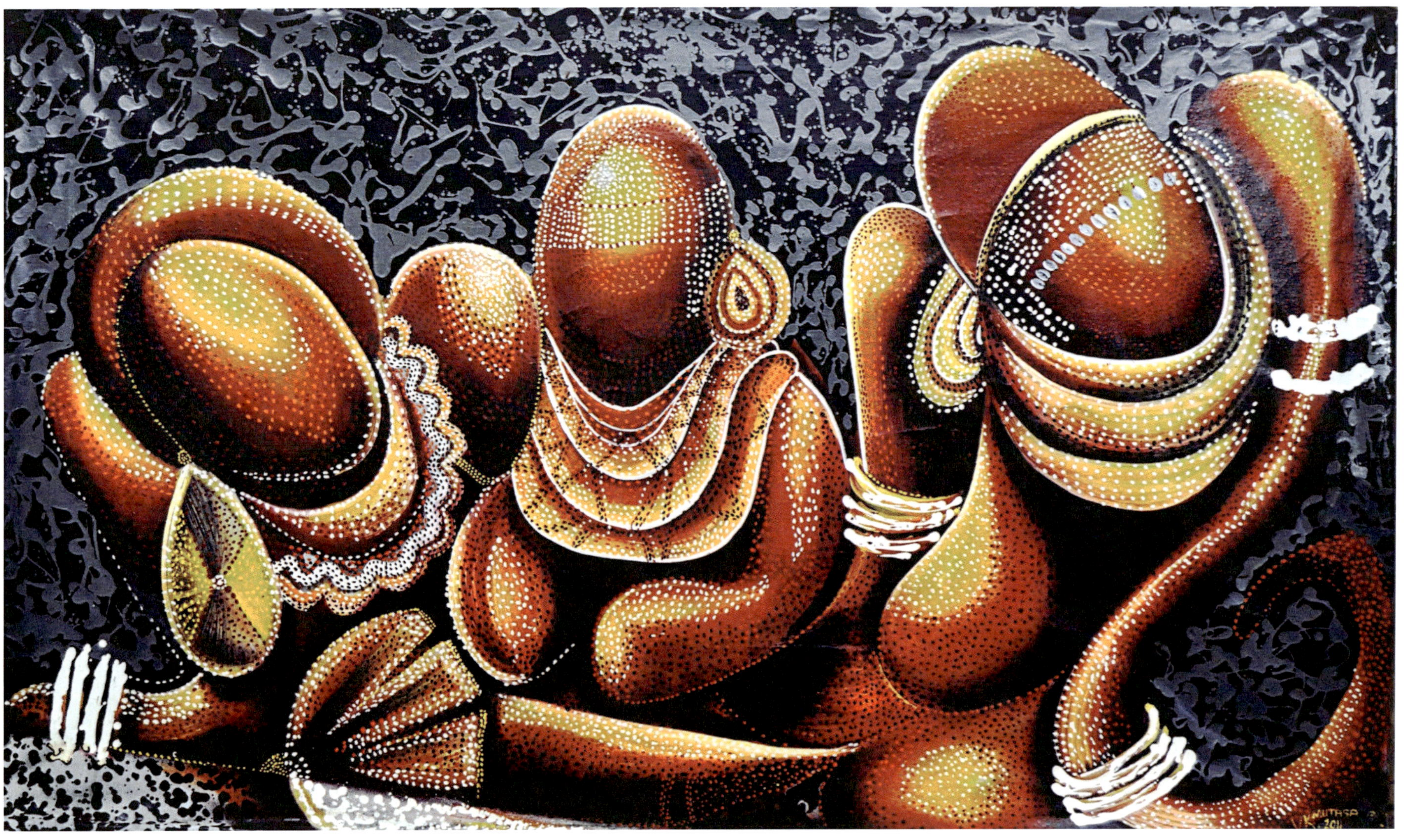

Sisterhood #1   V093   104 x 178 cm   (41" x 68")

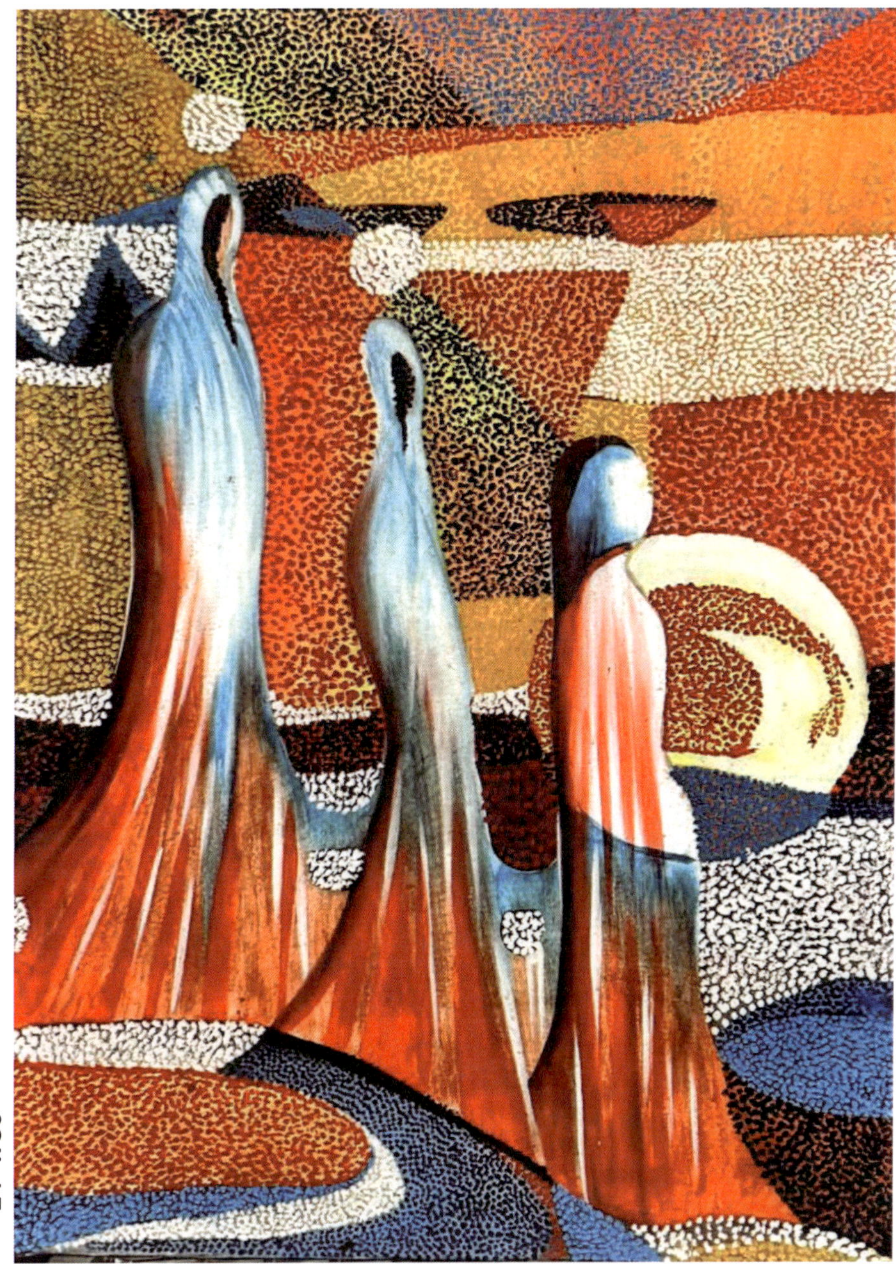

V20237
61 x 91 cm

Pointillism Oil
On Canvas

24" x 30"

Prayer For Peace

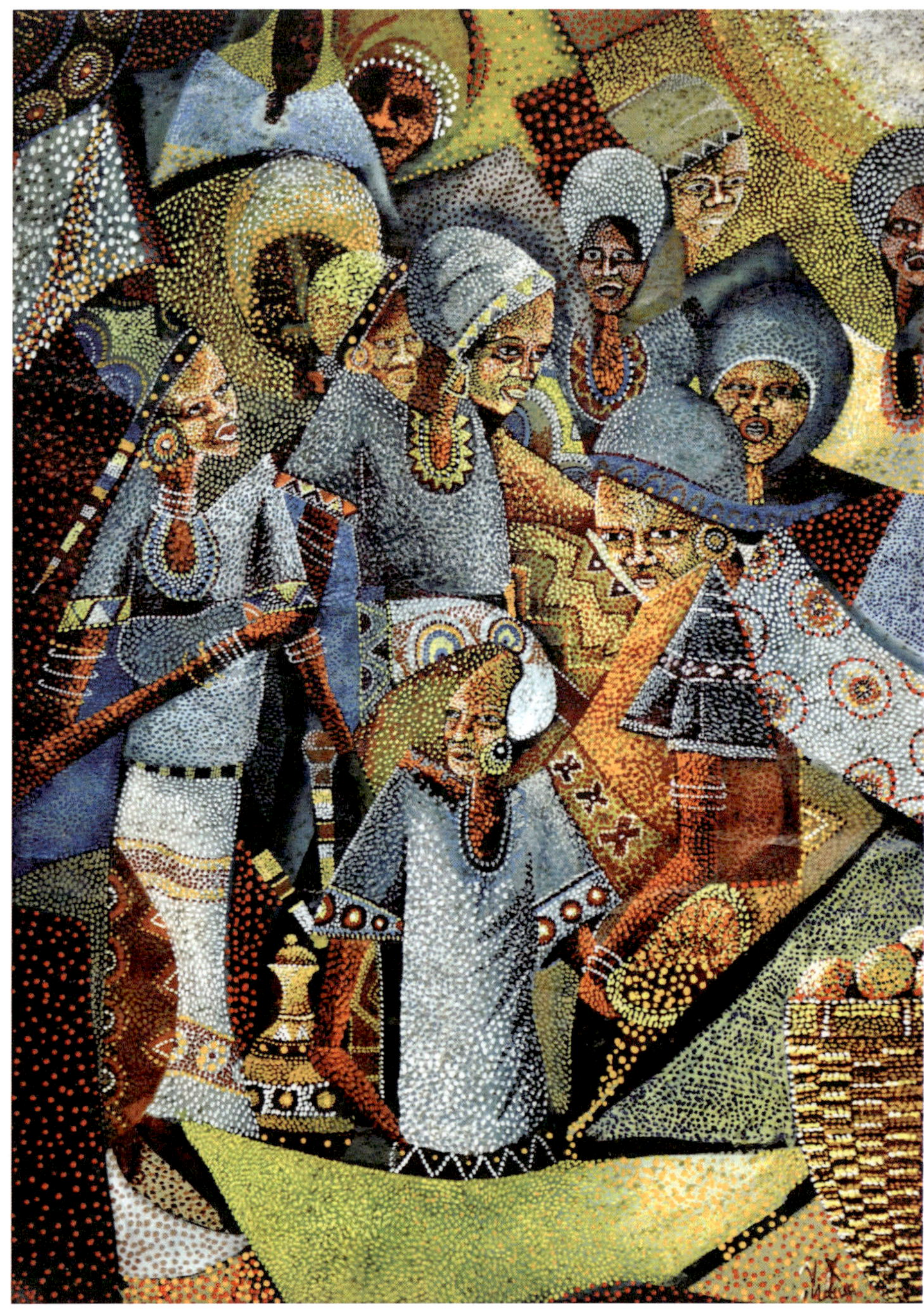

VKM—E007
88 x 122cm

Pointillism Oil
On Canvas

34" x 48"

Bearing Witness

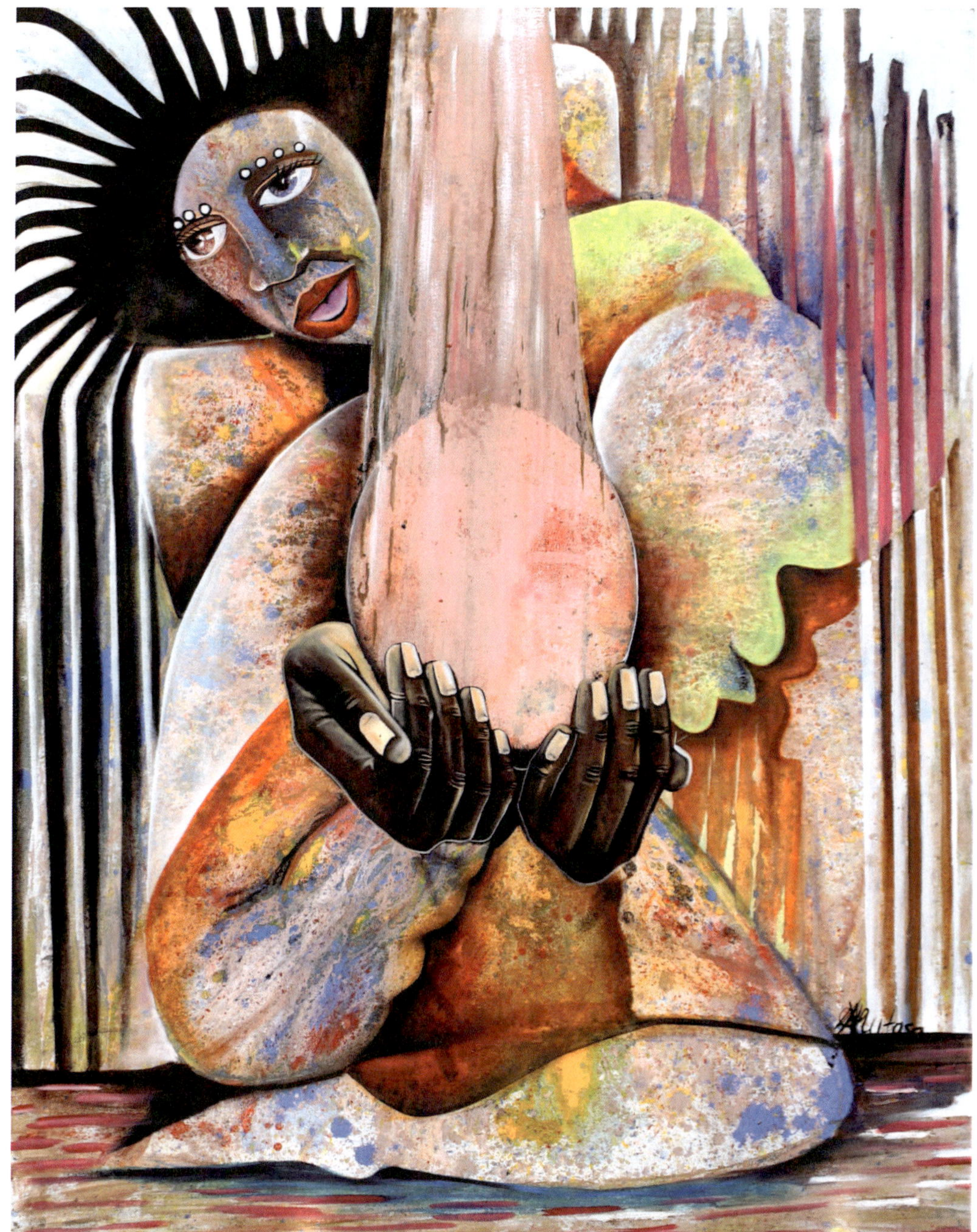

V20238
91 x 123cm

36" x 48"

Earth Mother Warrior Spirit #3

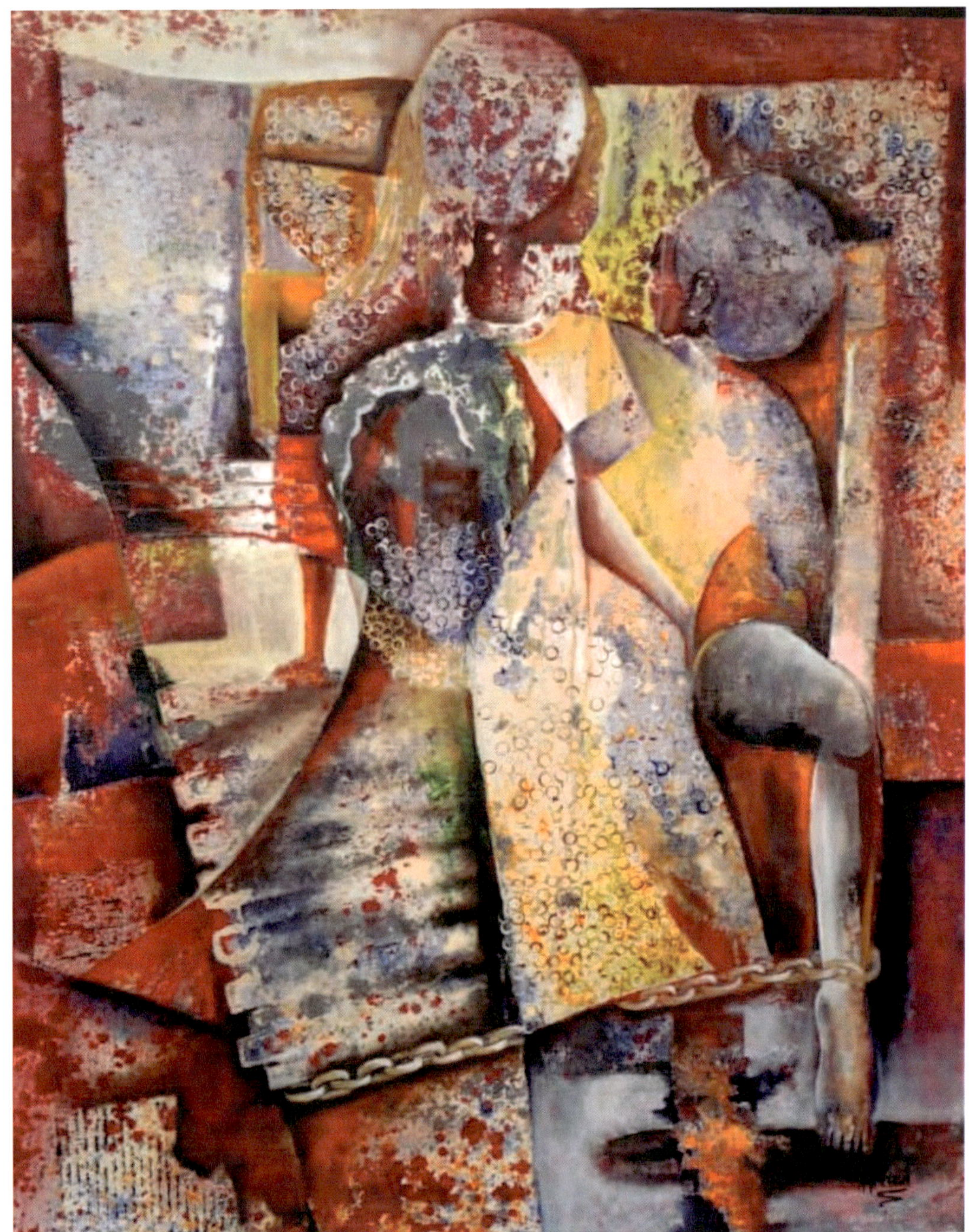

V20239
91 x 123cm

36" x 48"

Displaced

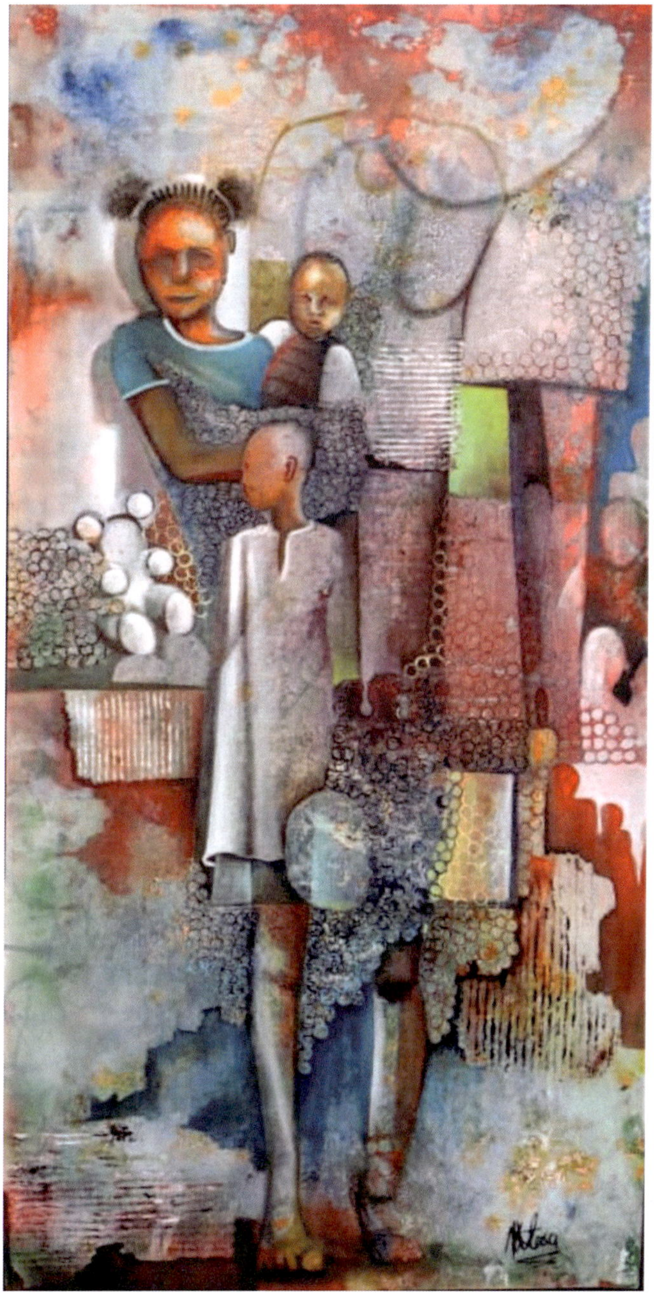

V202310
62 x 123cm

24" x 48"

Waiting

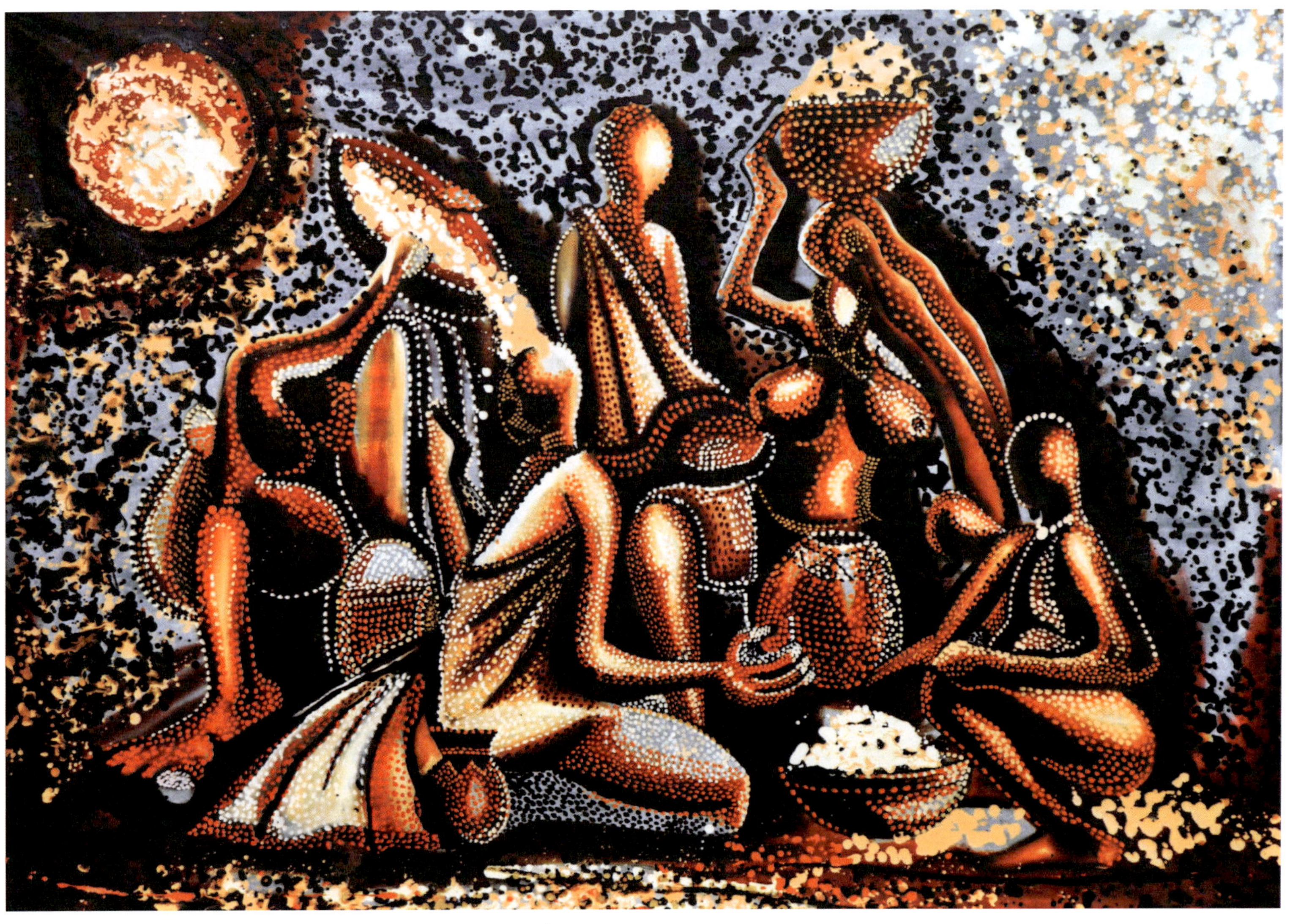

Sisterhood #2   VKM— E005   **142 x 109 cm   (55" x 43"**

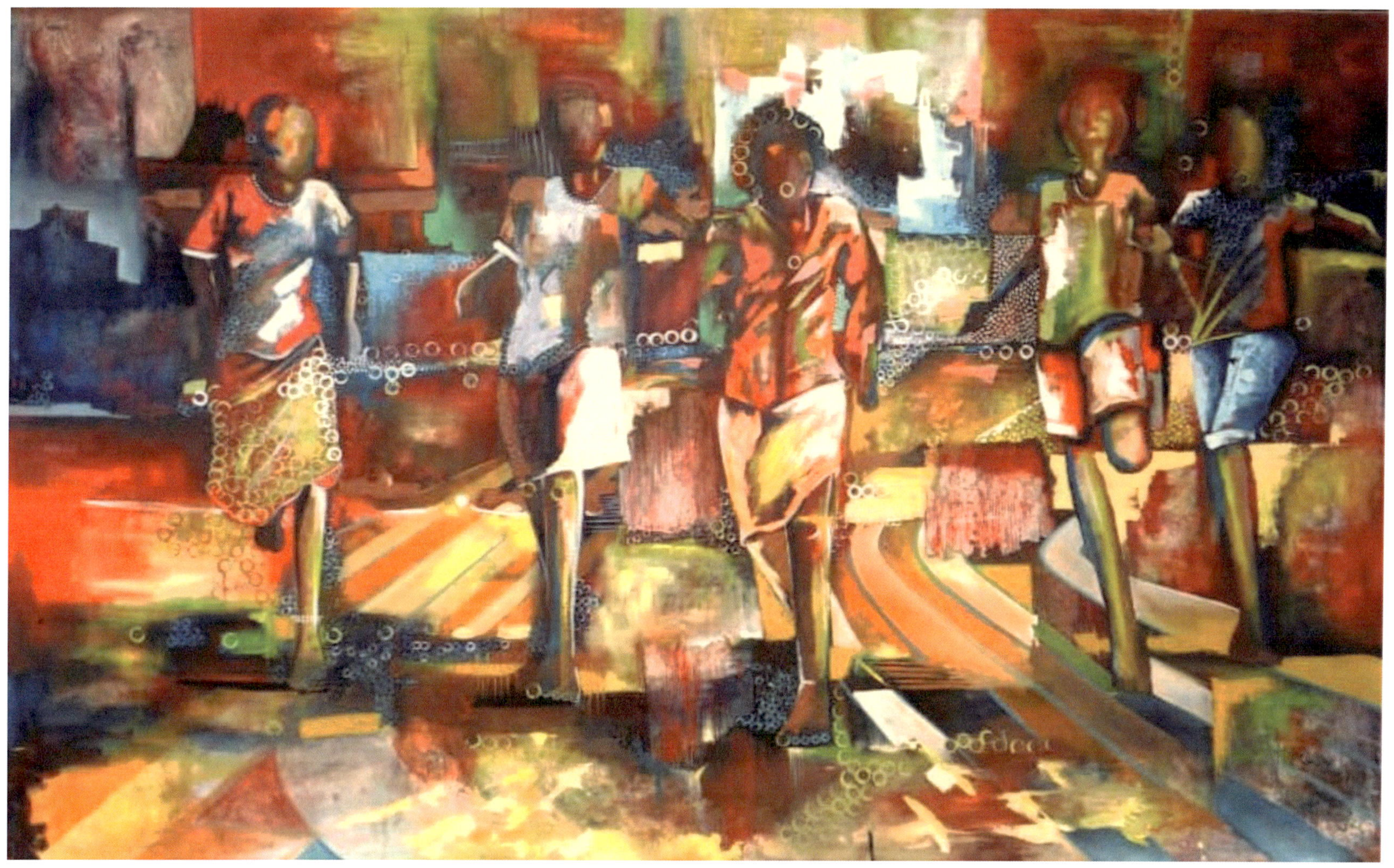

V202311   *Running The Same Race*   248 x 156 cm (97" x 61")

Artist Note: The women in the painting are all one –legged, depicting the disadvantage women start with in competition with men in society.

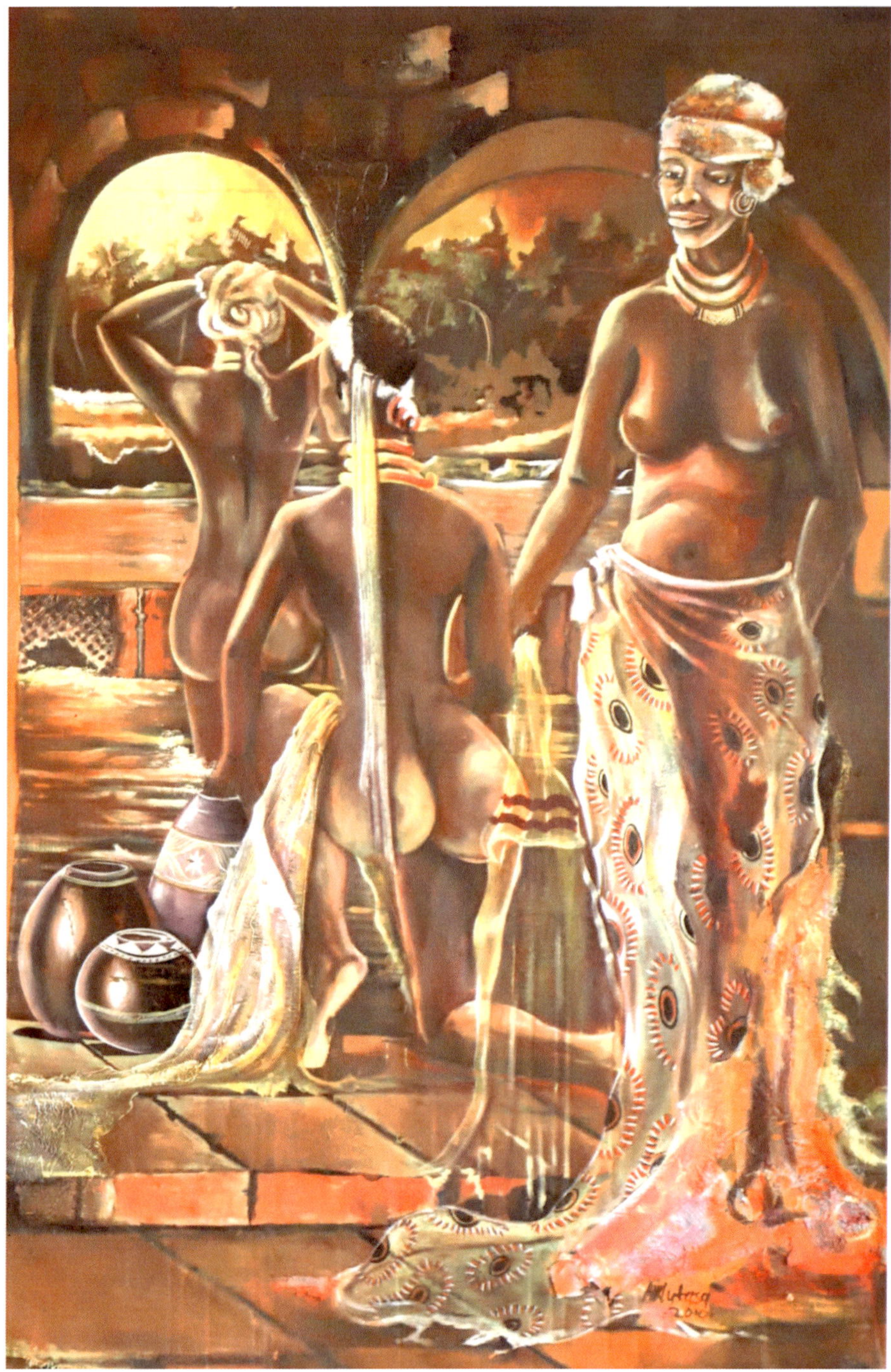

VKM—E009
93 x 131 cm

36" x 51"

Kurukova (At The River)

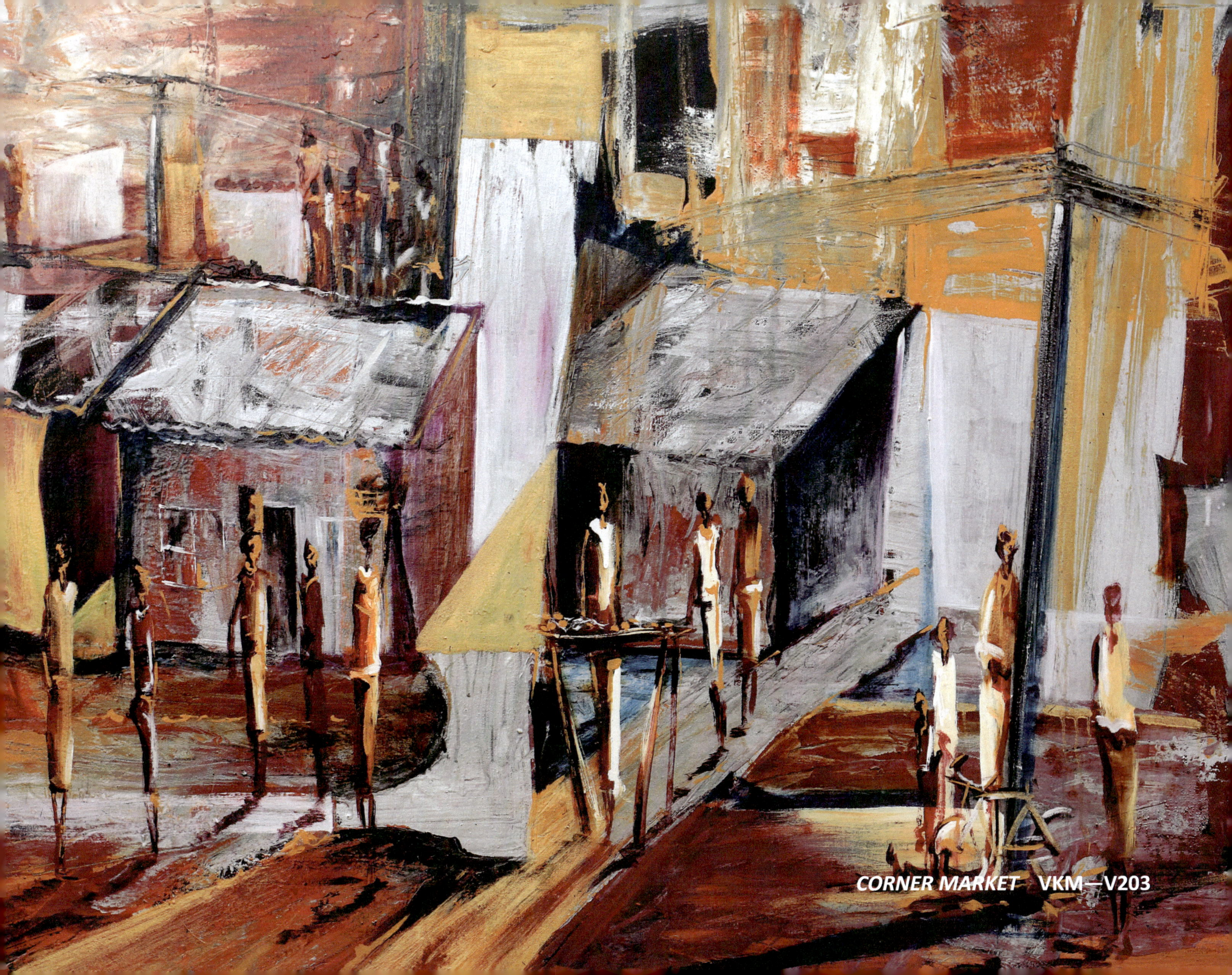
CORNER MARKET   VKM—V203

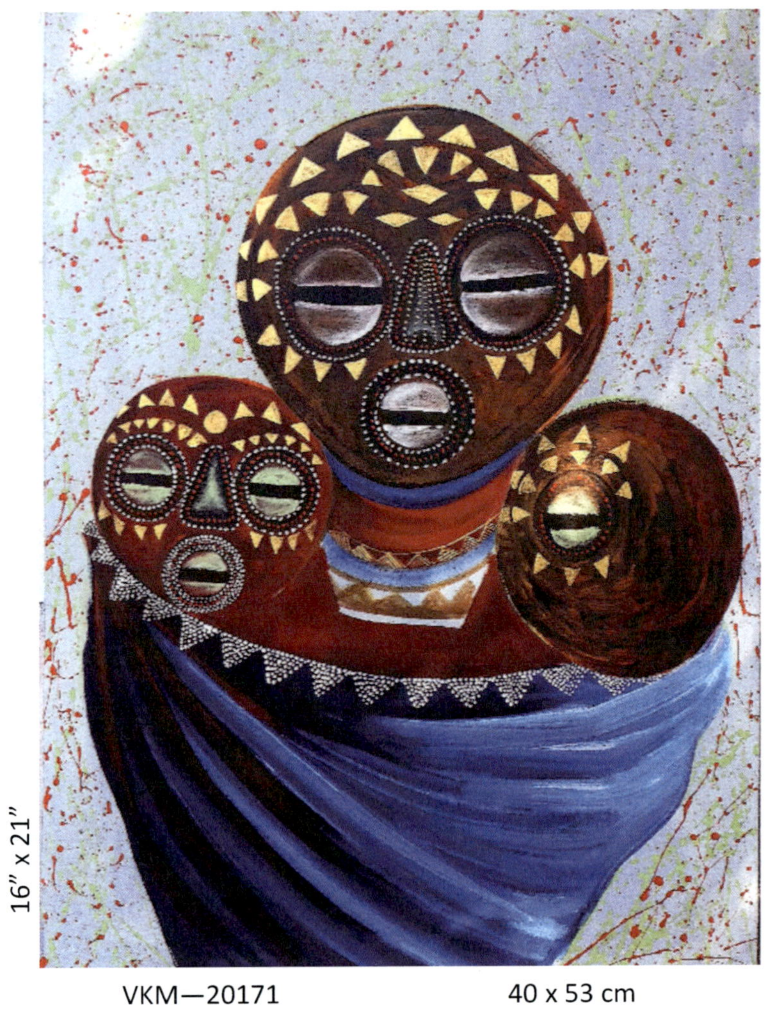

16" x 21"

VKM—20171   40 x 53 cm

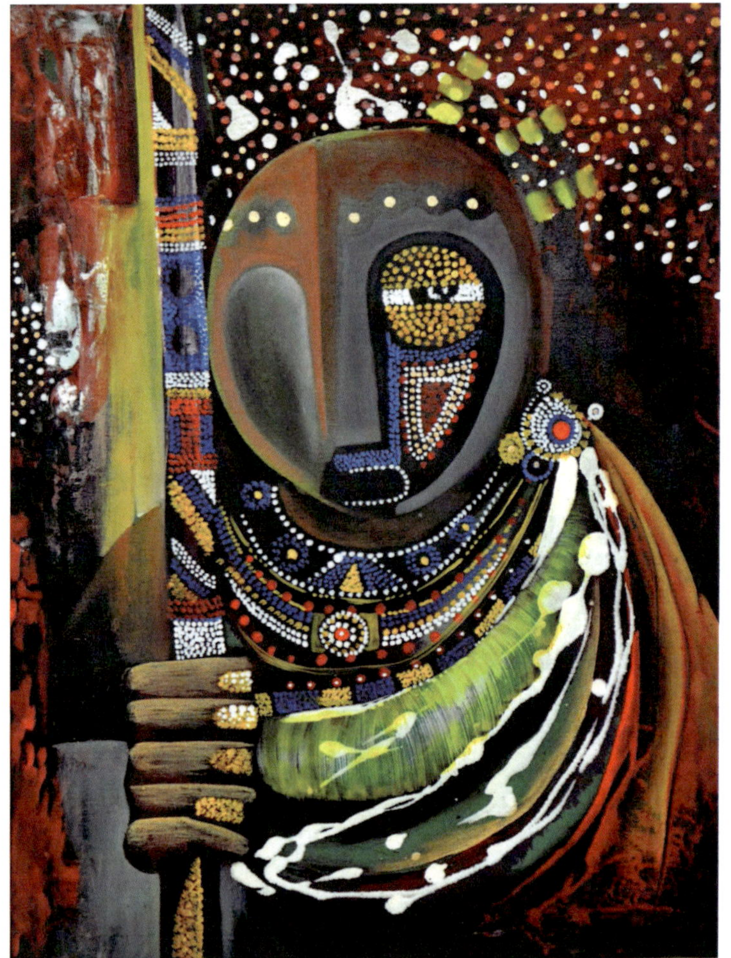

18" x 24"

VKM— V031   45 x 61cm

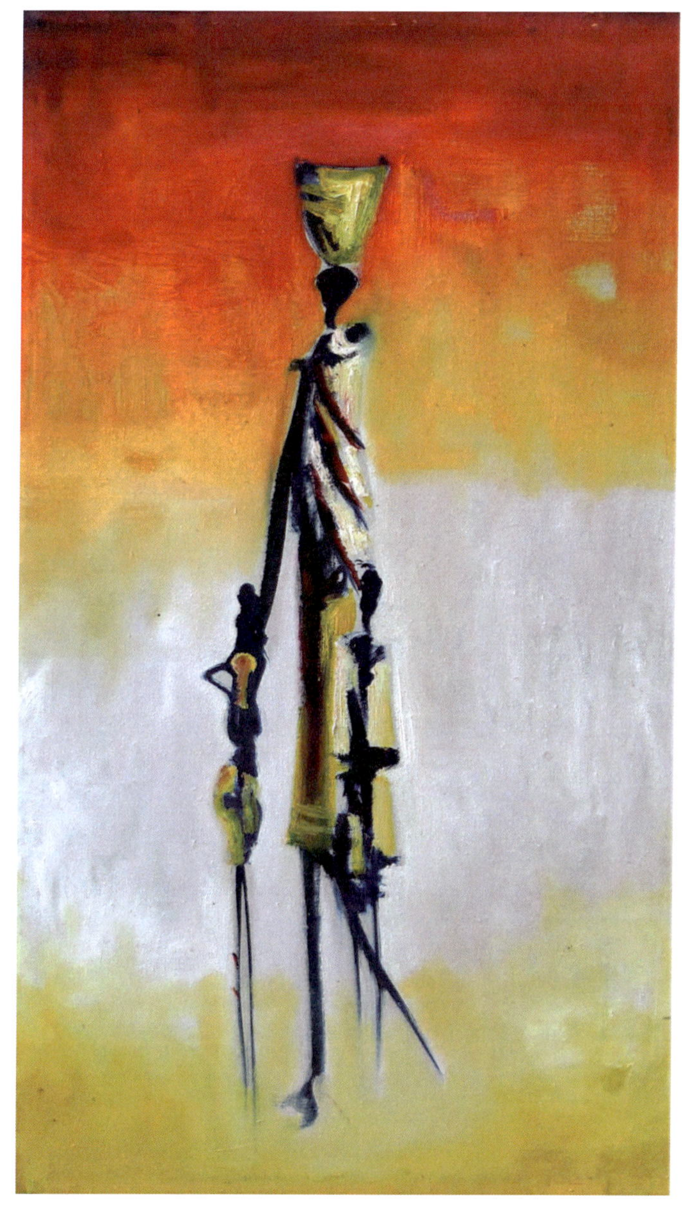

VKM—20172   40 x 61cm

16" x 24"

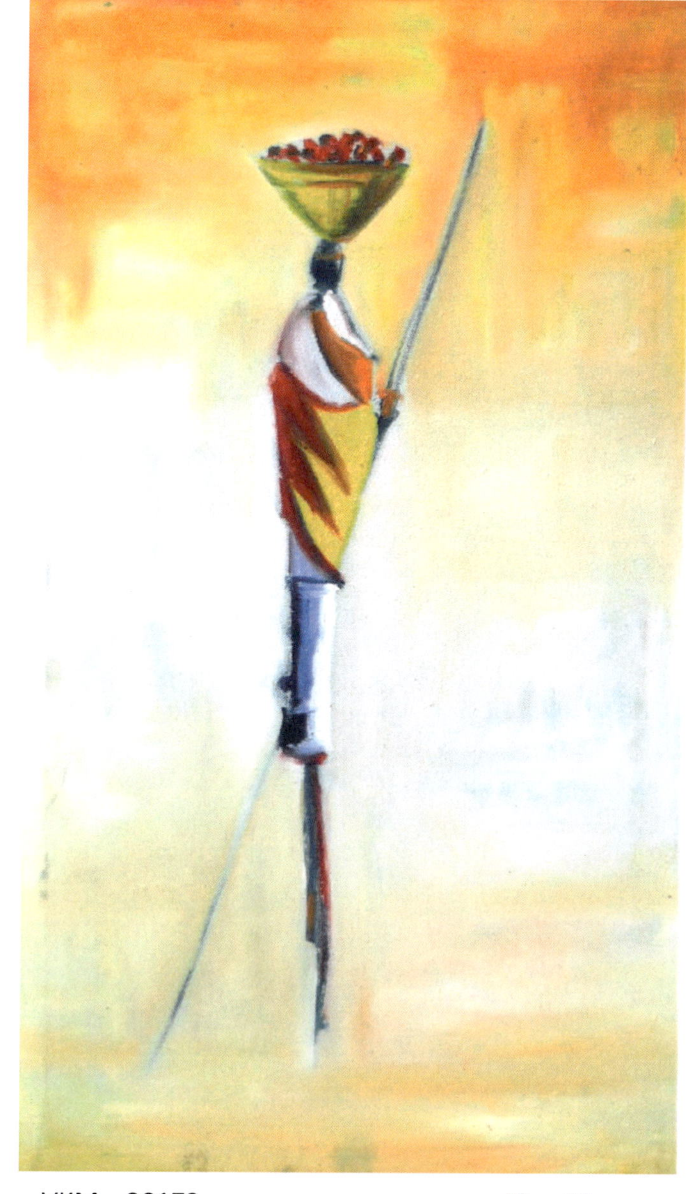

VKM—20173   40 x 61cm

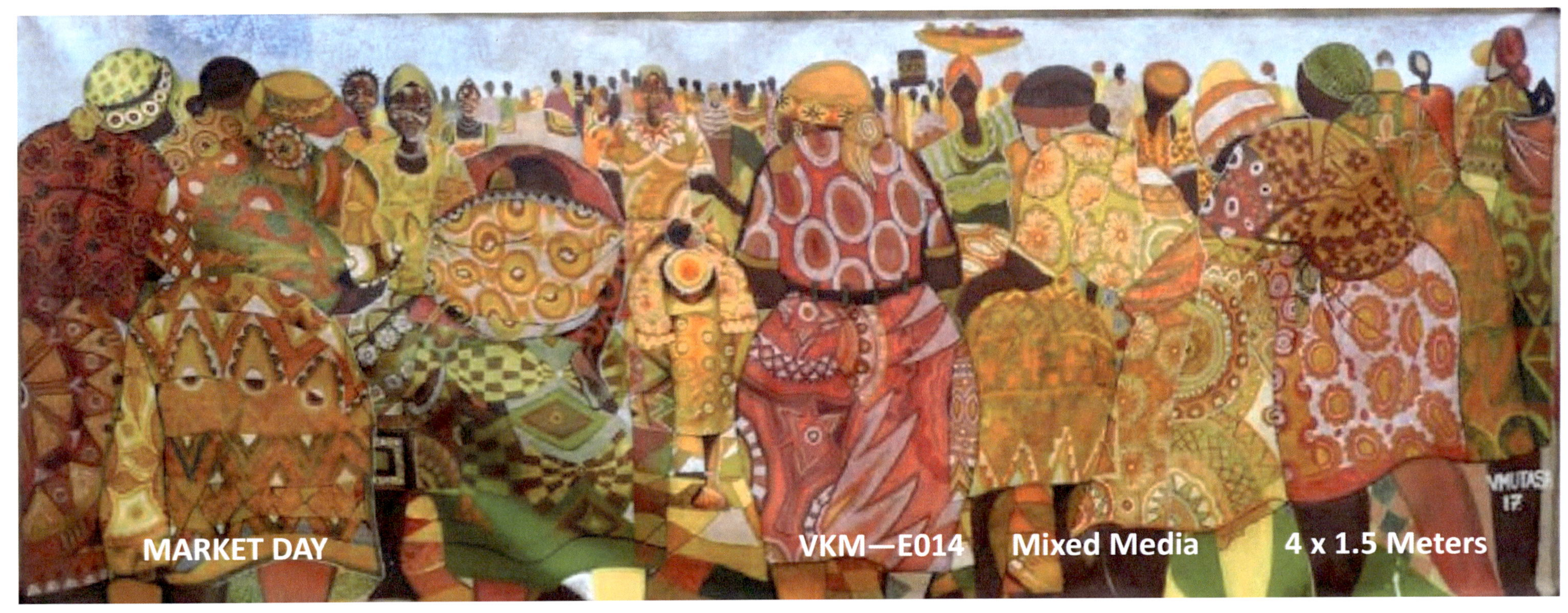

MARKET DAY
VKM—E014   Mixed Media   4 x 1.5 Meters

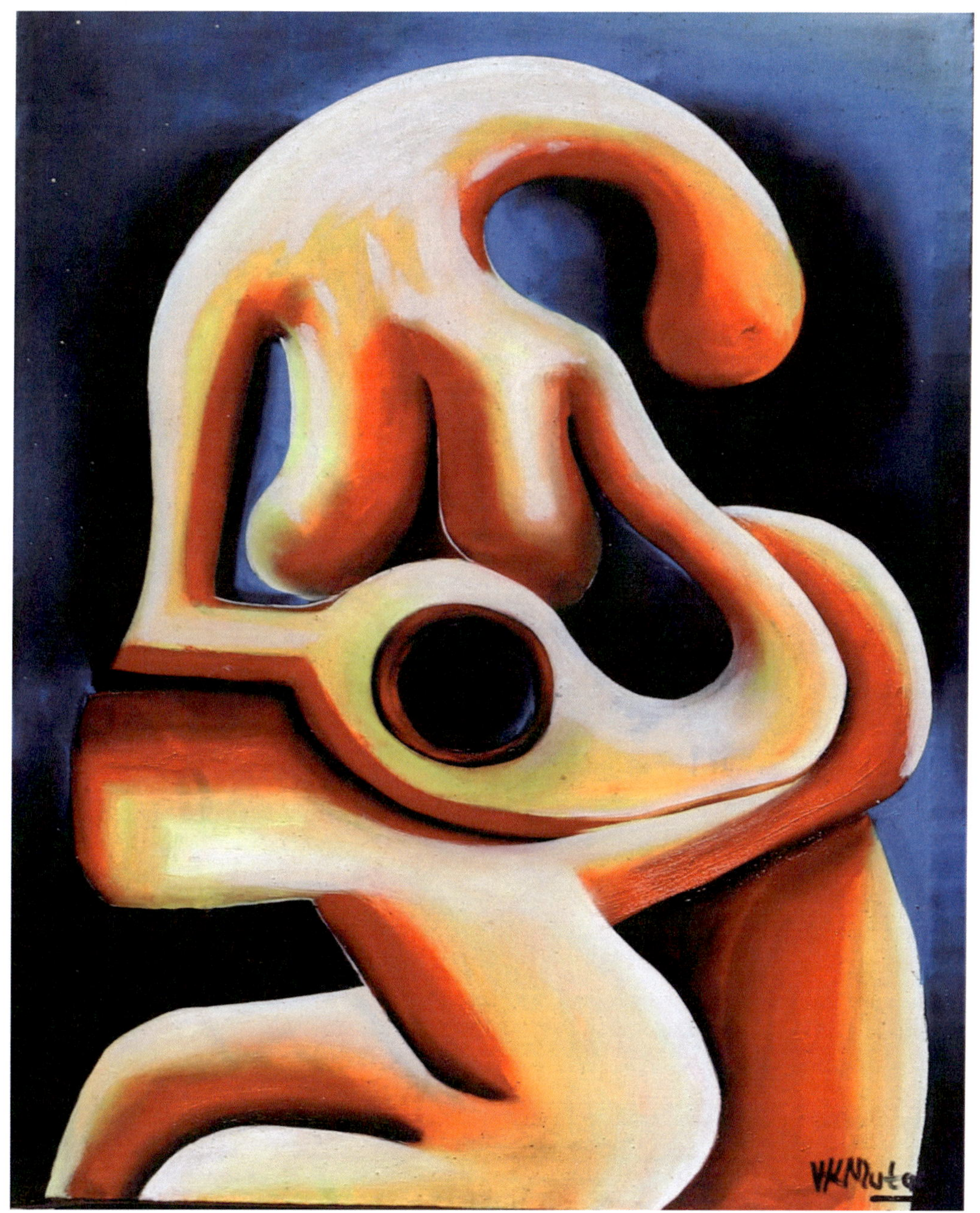

91 x 123cm (36" x 48")

Mother's Milk

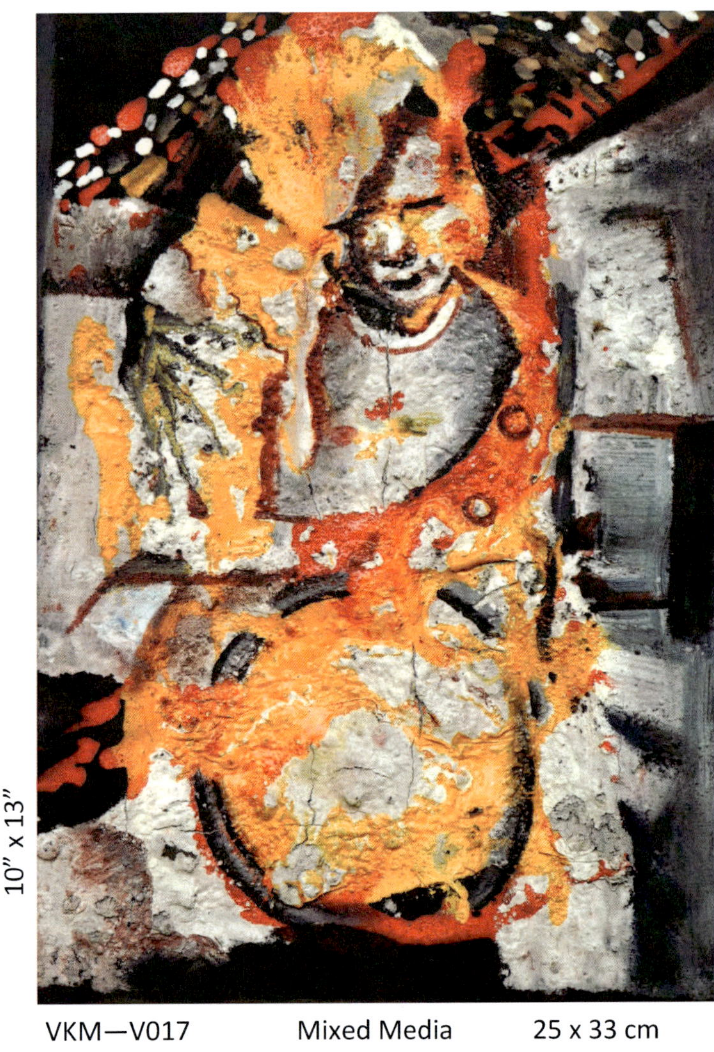

10" x 13"

VKM—V017   Mixed Media   25 x 33 cm

Witness to a
CHANGED CLIMATE

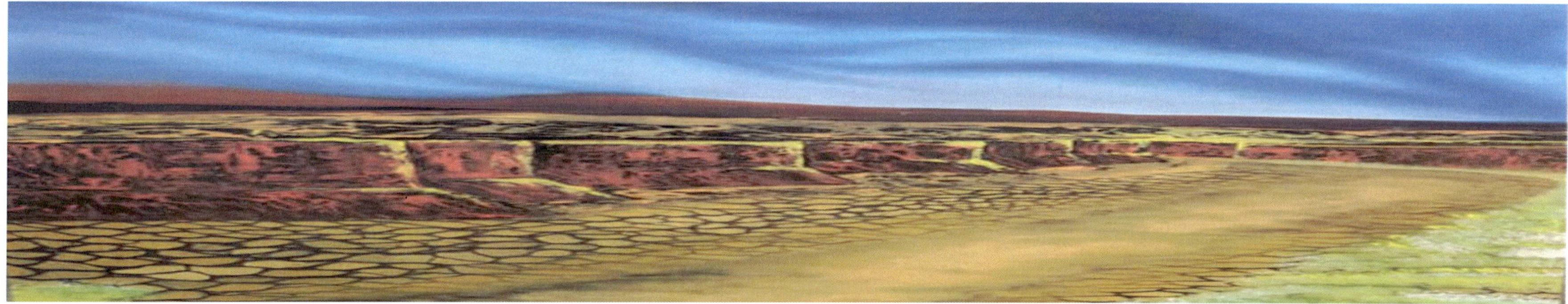

The phenomenon known as 'global warning' has become a lived experience across AFRICA. The African continent, which has contributed the least to cause the problem of global warning has borne the heaviest brunt of the changing climate.

Valentine's paintings are a reflection on the cataclysmic consequences of the changed climate which has come with prolonged periods of drought, destructive flooding and wild fires ravaging the landscape, displacing man and beast.

- Except were indicated, all artworks are oil on canvass. The pictorial presentation of the artworks is for representation and information purposes only. Where possible the actual size of the artwork is listed with the artwork.

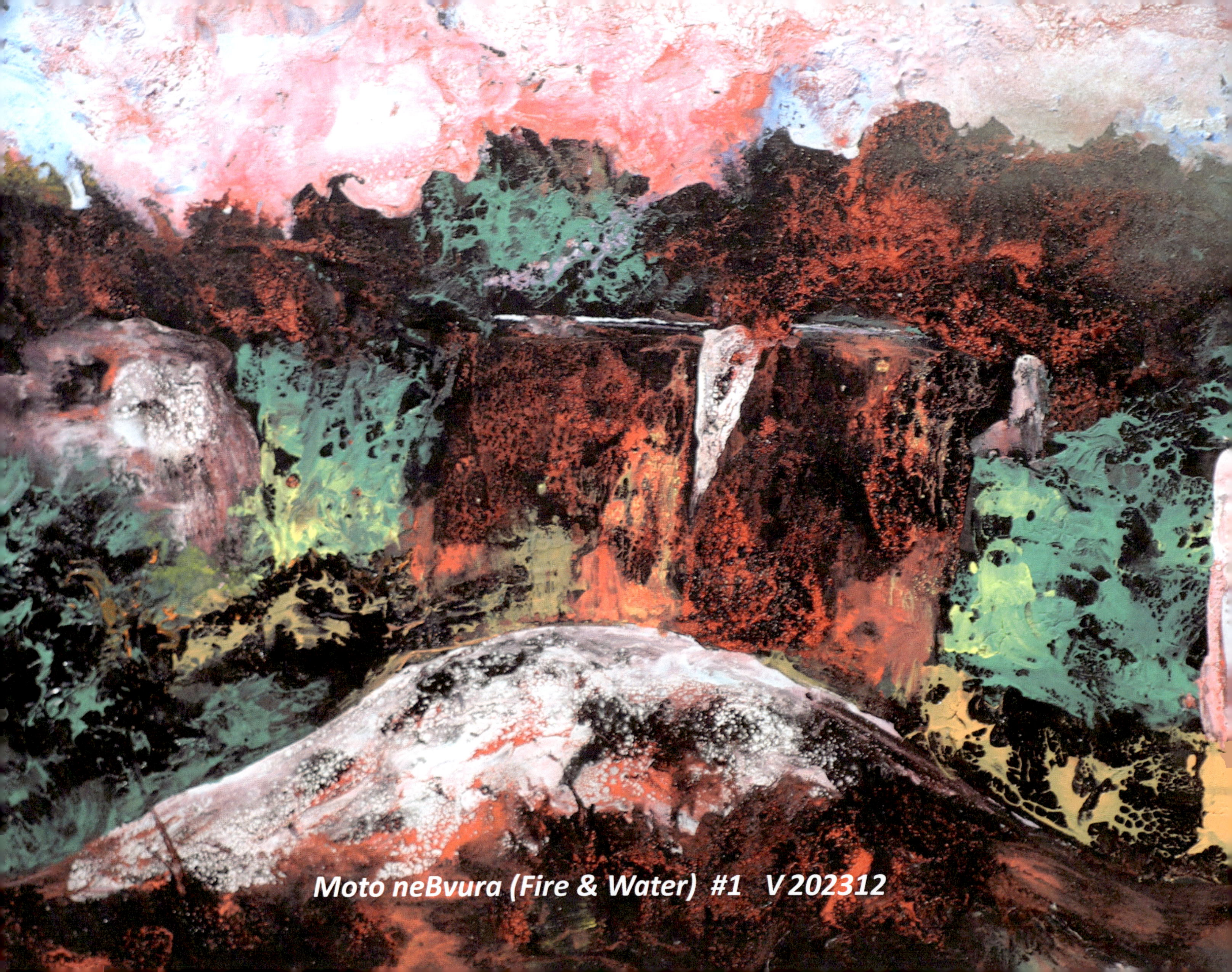

Moto neBvura (Fire & Water) #1   V 202312

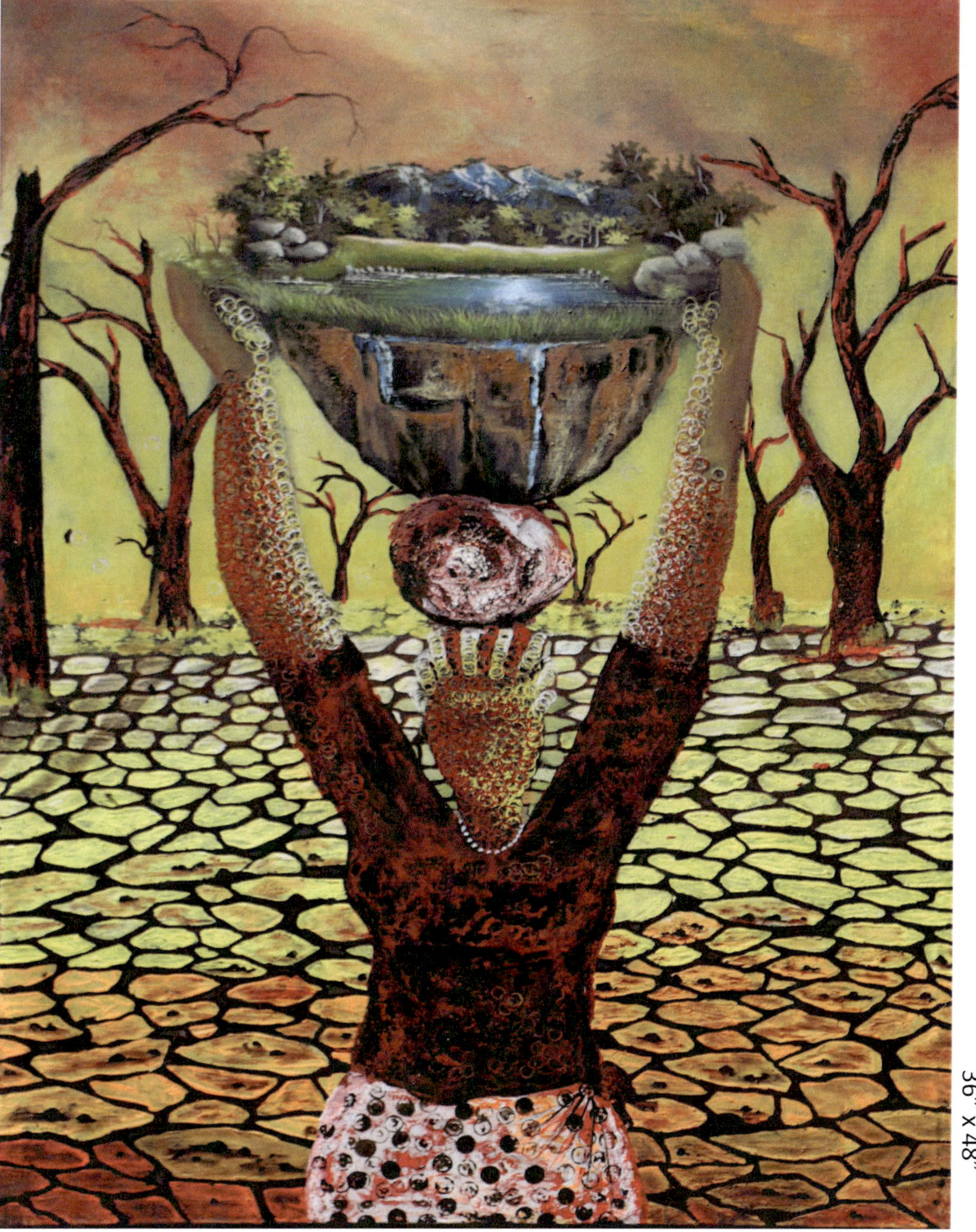

V202314
91 x 123cm

36" x 48"

Fruit Basket From The Industrial Revolution

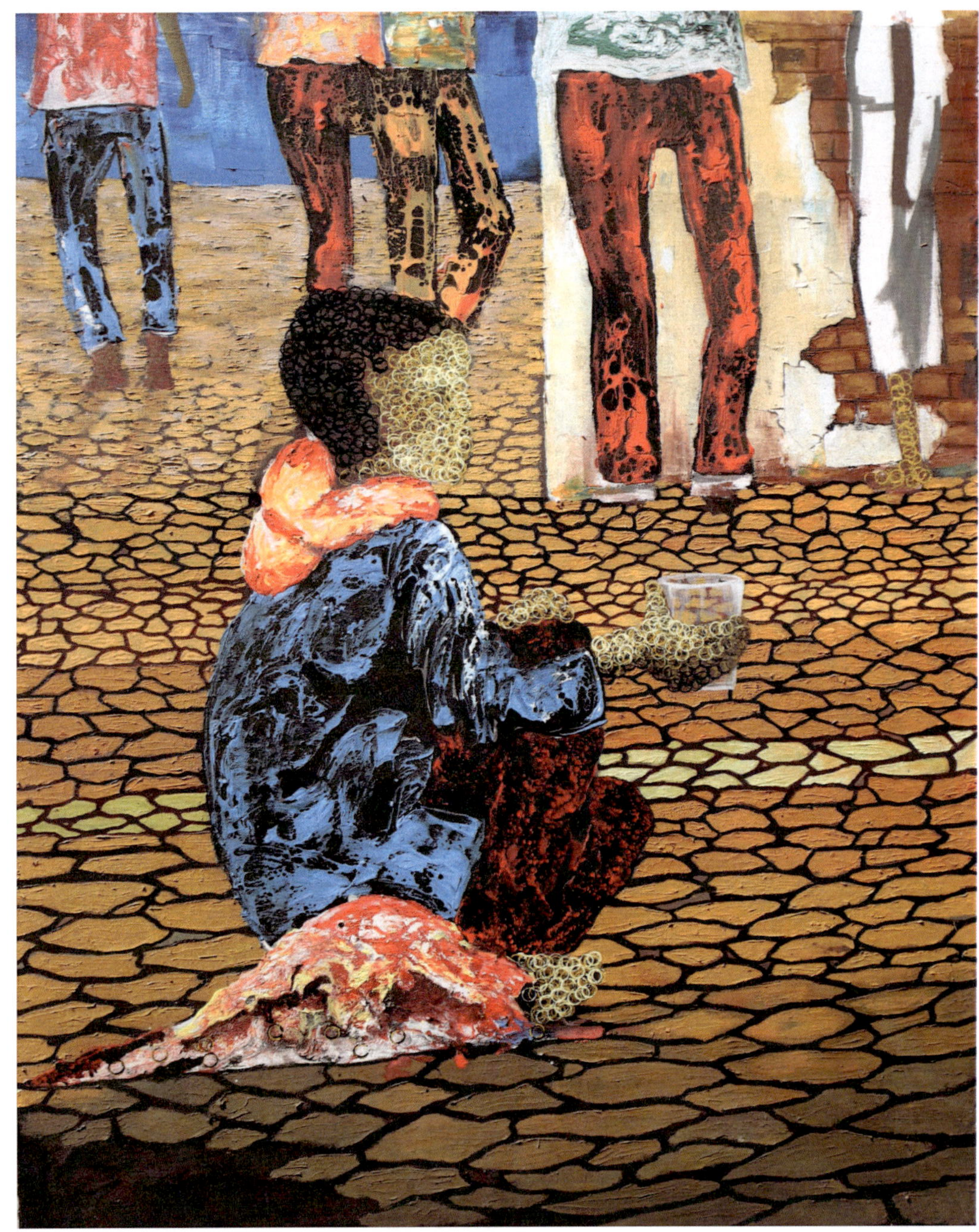

V202313
91 x 123cm

36" x 48"

Water Beggar Boy

V202315
91 x 123cm

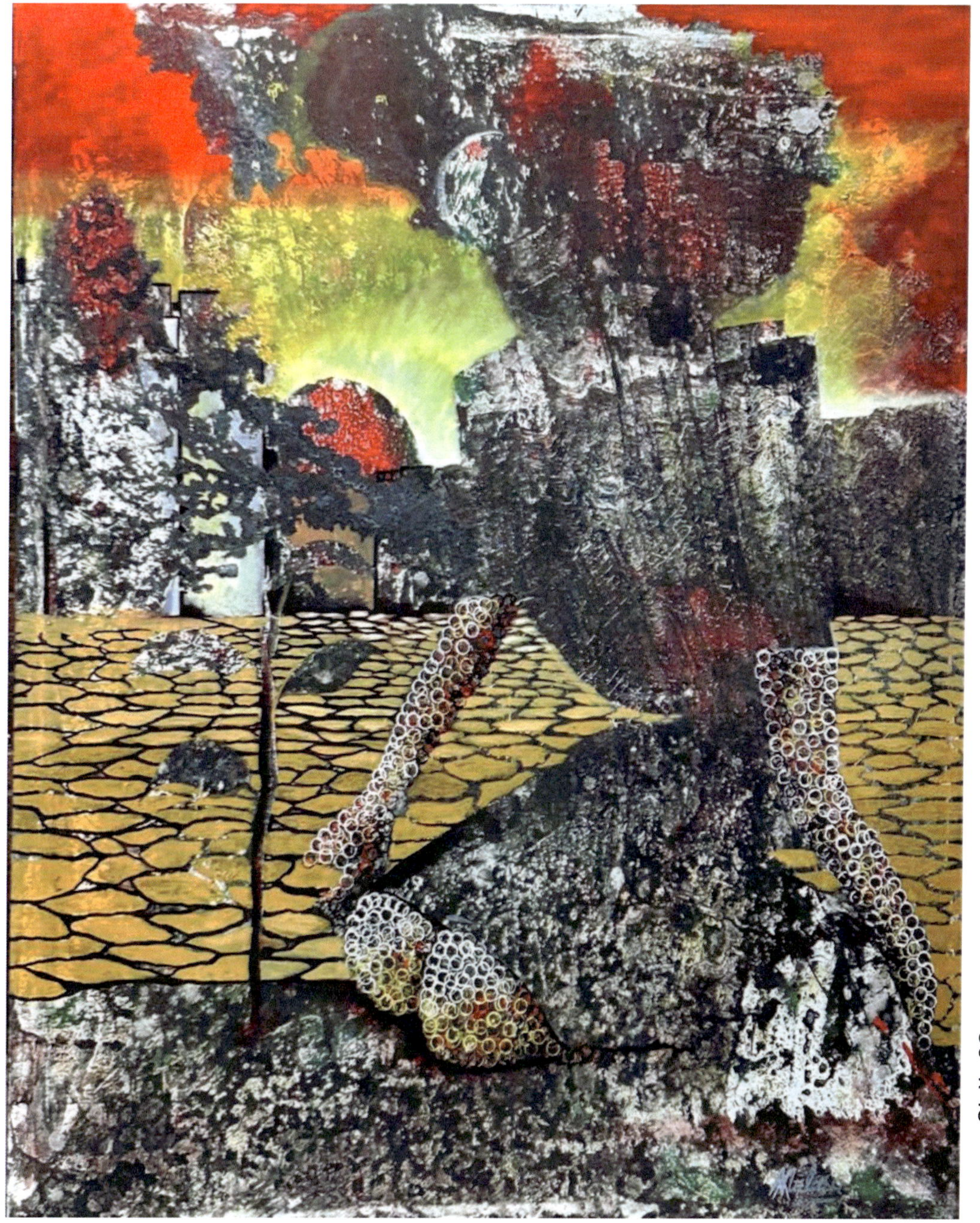

36" x 48"

The Last Gardner

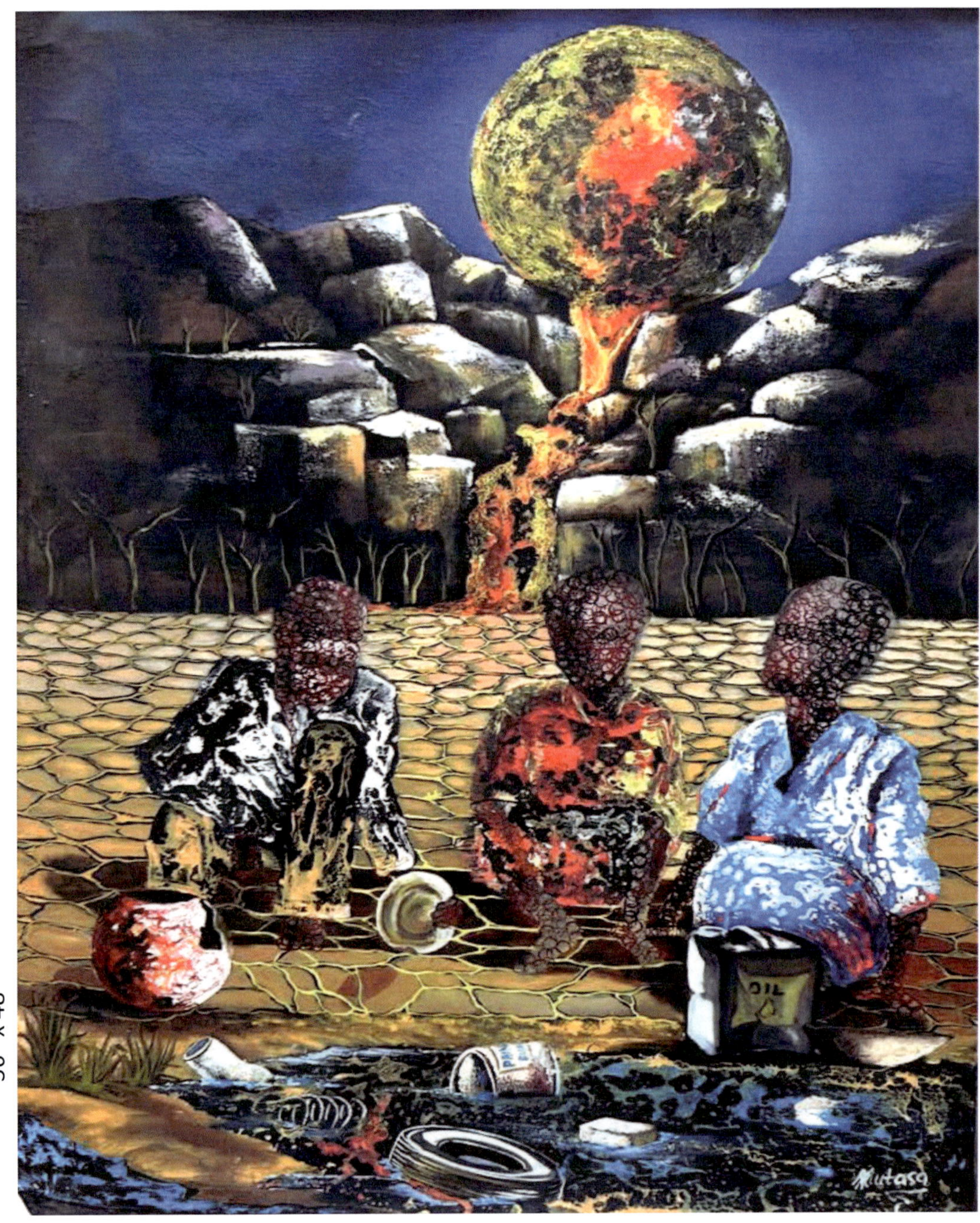

V202316
91 x 123cm

36" x 48"

Times Past Remembered

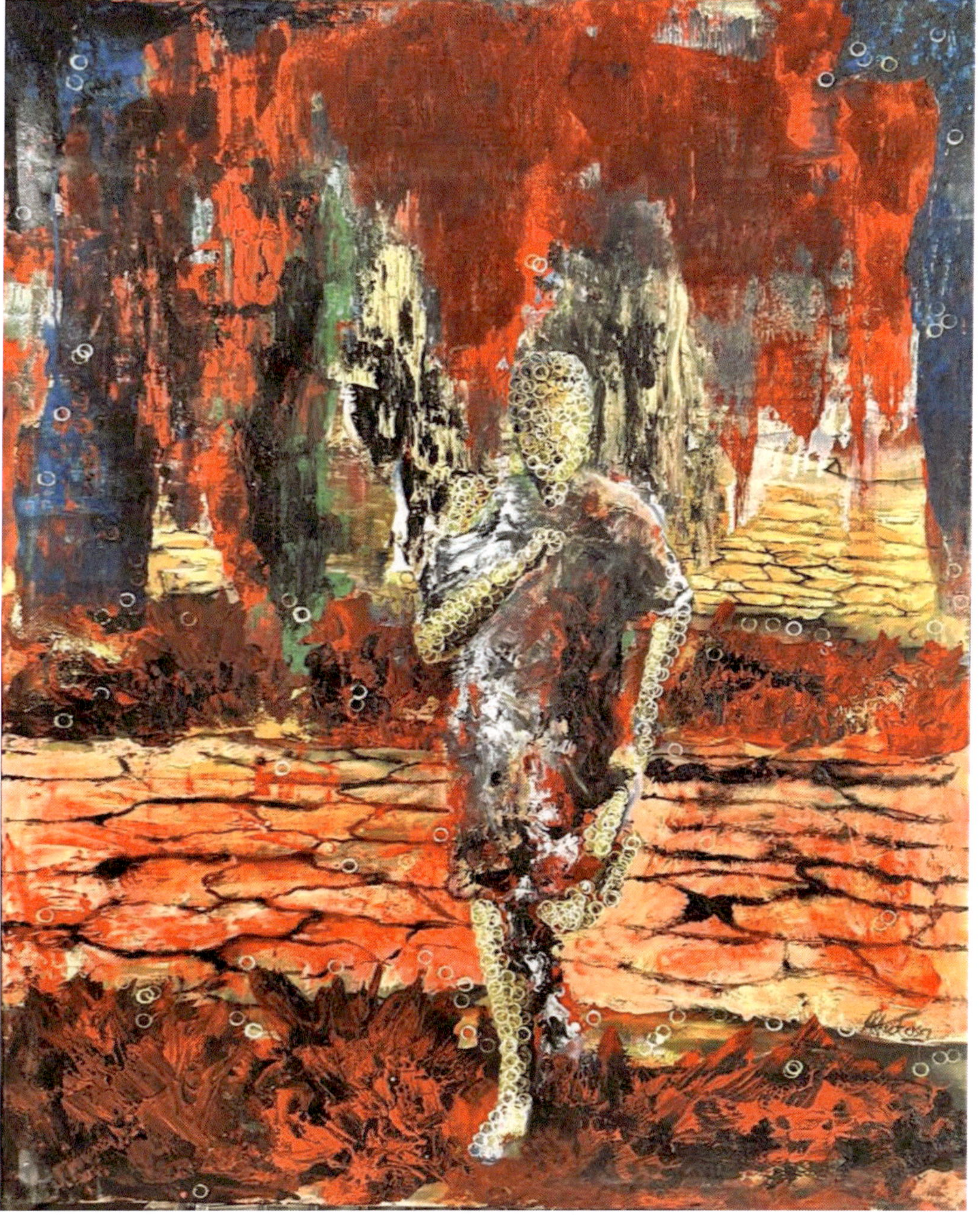

V202317
91 x 123cm

36" x 48"

Flight From Our Future

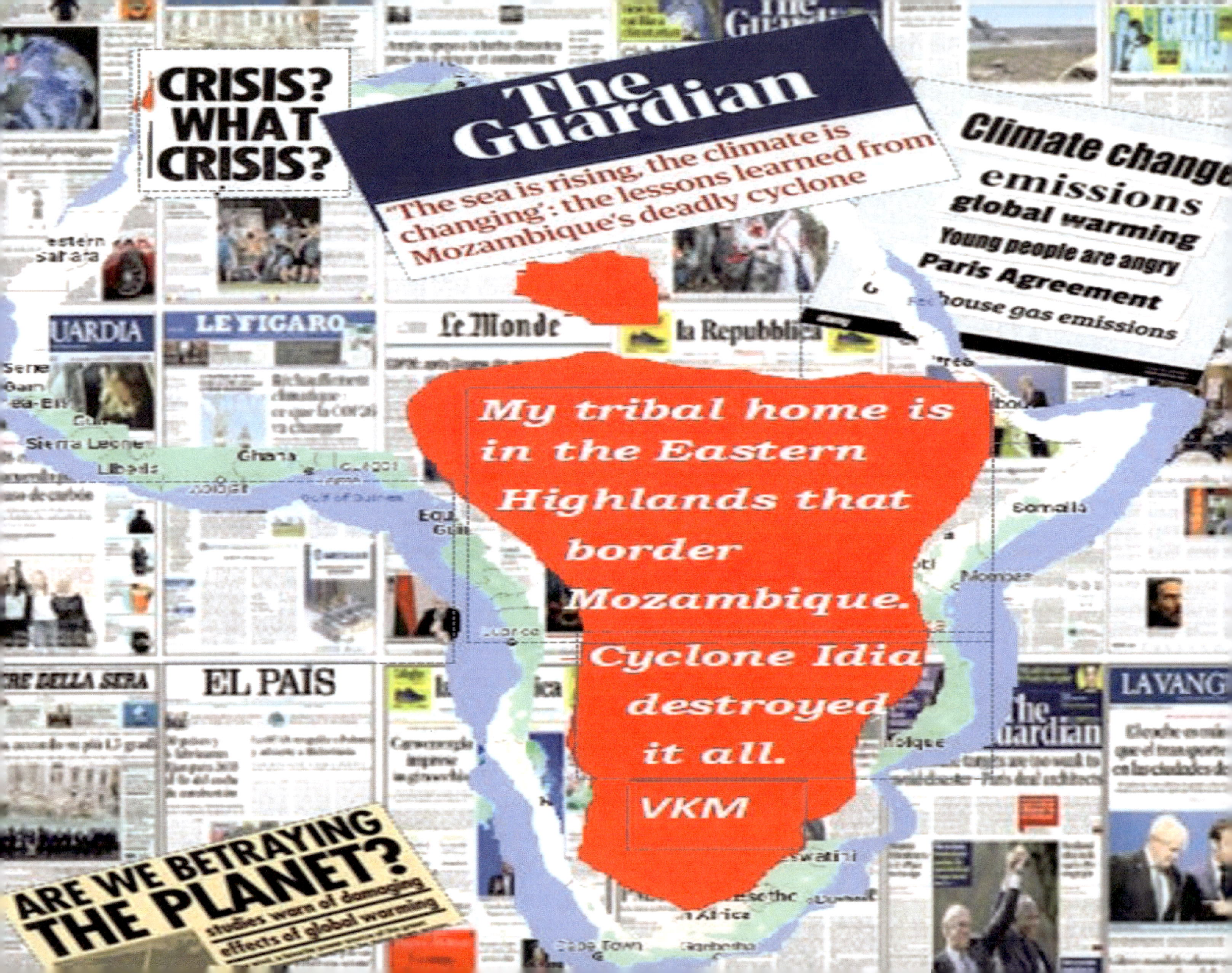

CRISIS? WHAT CRISIS?
The Guardian
'The sea is rising, the climate is changing': the lessons learned from Mozambique's deadly cyclone
Climate change
emissions
global warming
Young people are angry
Paris Agreement
greenhouse gas emissions
LA GUARDIA
LE FIGARO
Le Monde
la Repubblica
CORRIERE DELLA SERA
EL PAÍS
LA VANGUARDIA
My tribal home is in the Eastern Highlands that border Mozambique. Cyclone Idia destroyed it all.
VKM
ARE WE BETRAYING THE PLANET?
studies warn of damaging effects of global warming

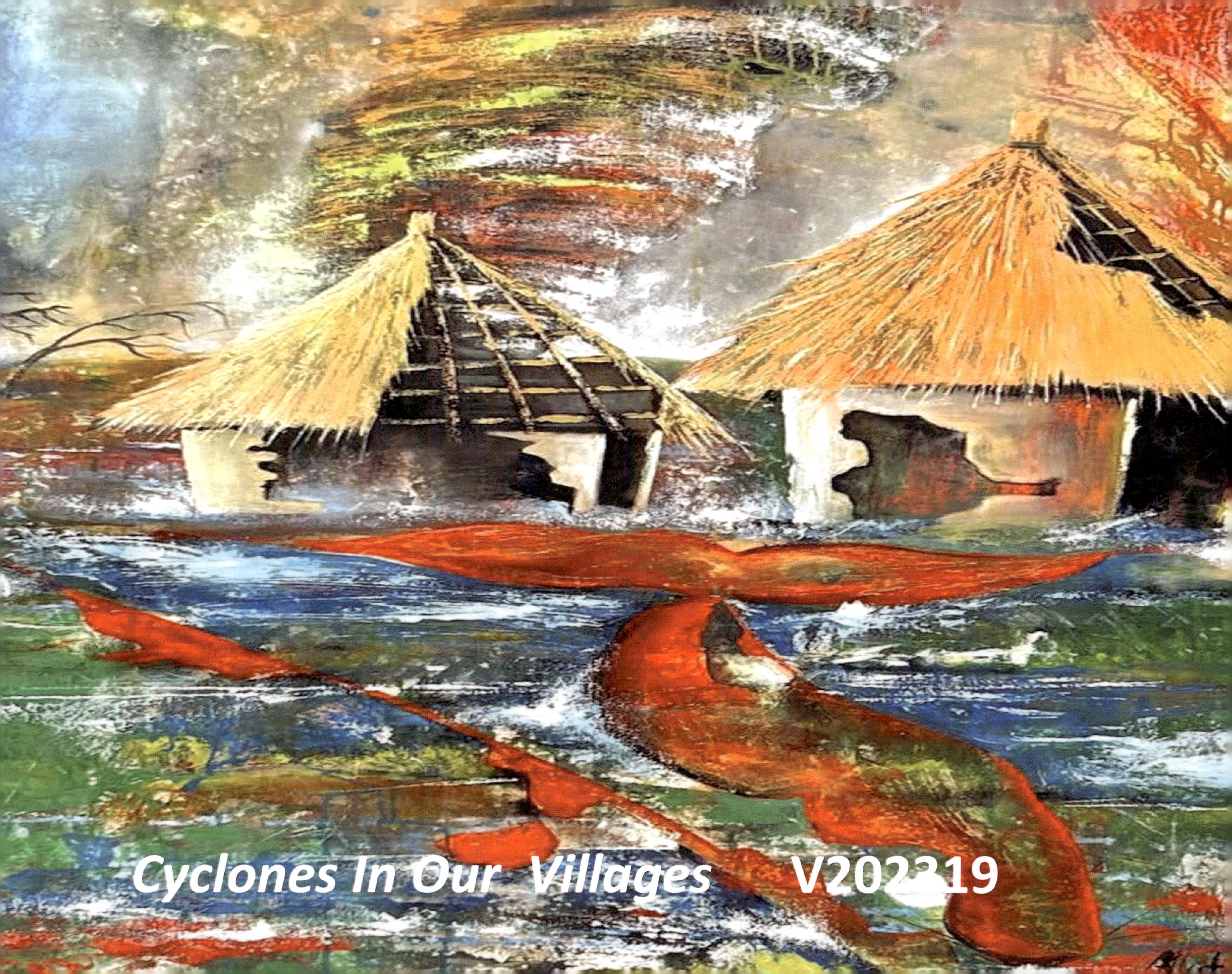

Cyclones In Our Villages   V202319

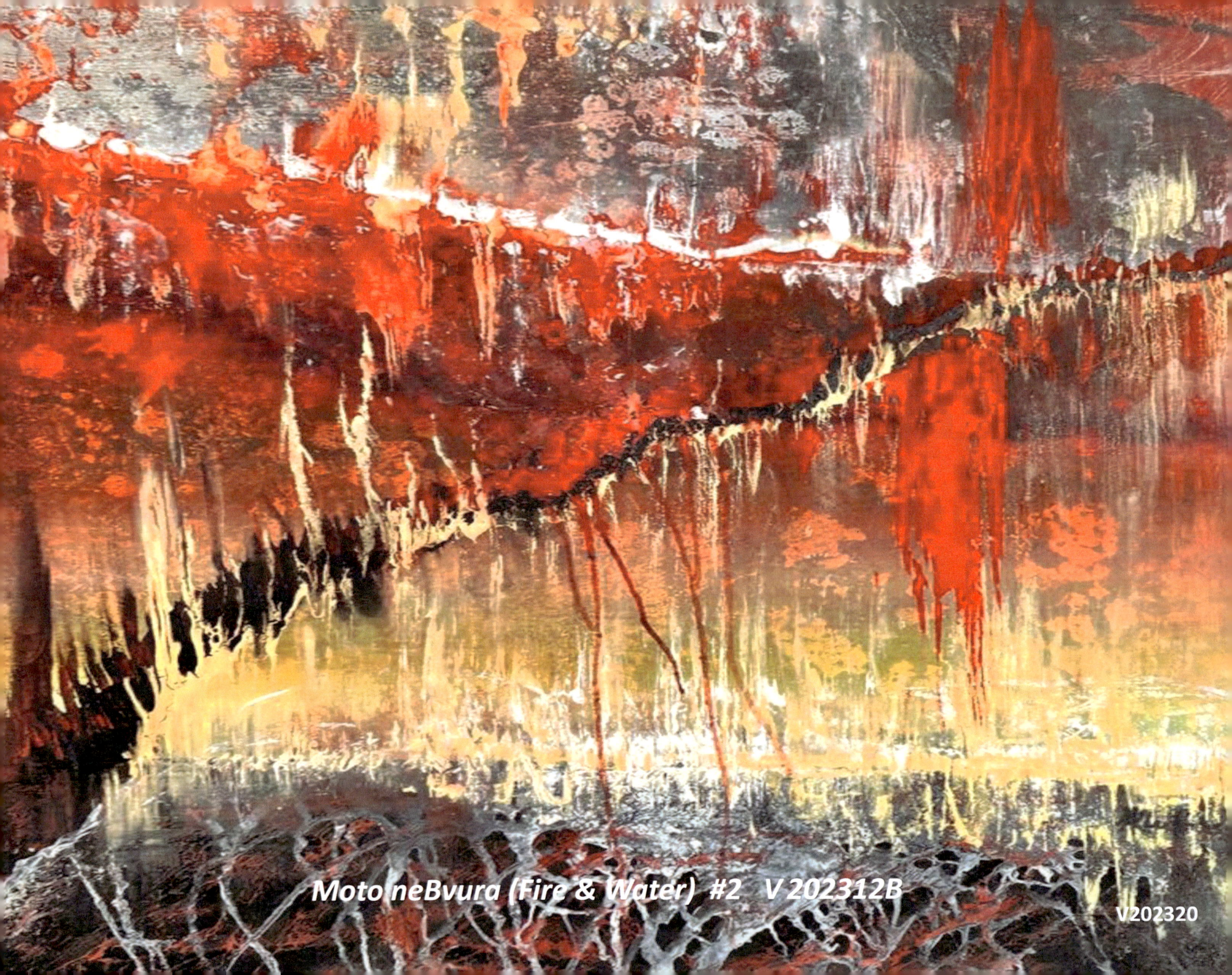

Moto neBvura (Fire & Water) #2   V 202312B
V202320

My Visions in Abstract Terms
2006 - 2020

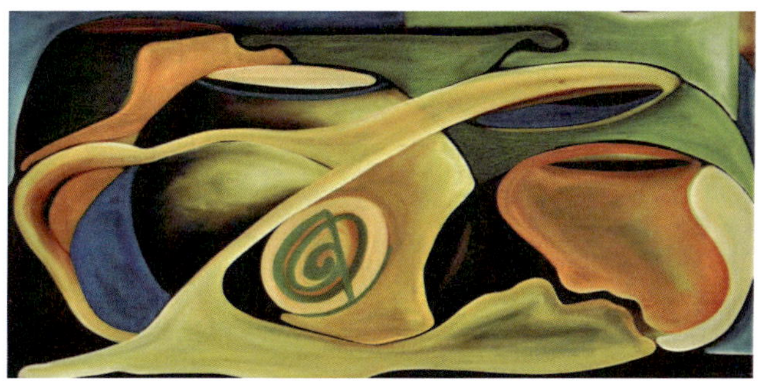

I belong with art. My spirit is restless when I am not creating new artworks. I paint and inspire myself knowing that where there is hope there is a future, and I am a very hopeful person.

- Except were indicated, all artworks are oil on canvass. The pictorial presentation of the artworks is for representation and information purposes only. Where possible the actual size of the artwork is listed with the artwork.

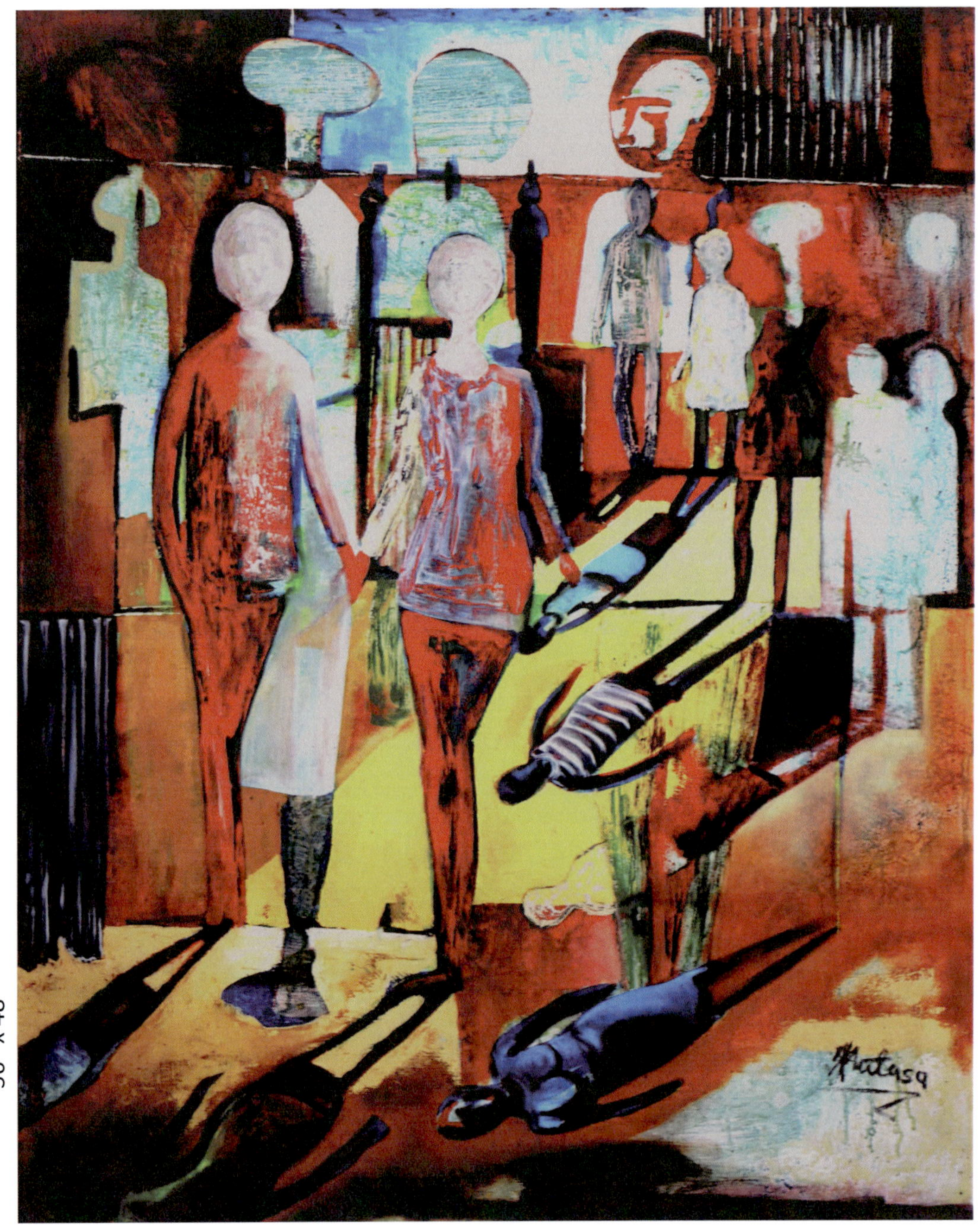

36" x 48"

V202321
91 x 123cm

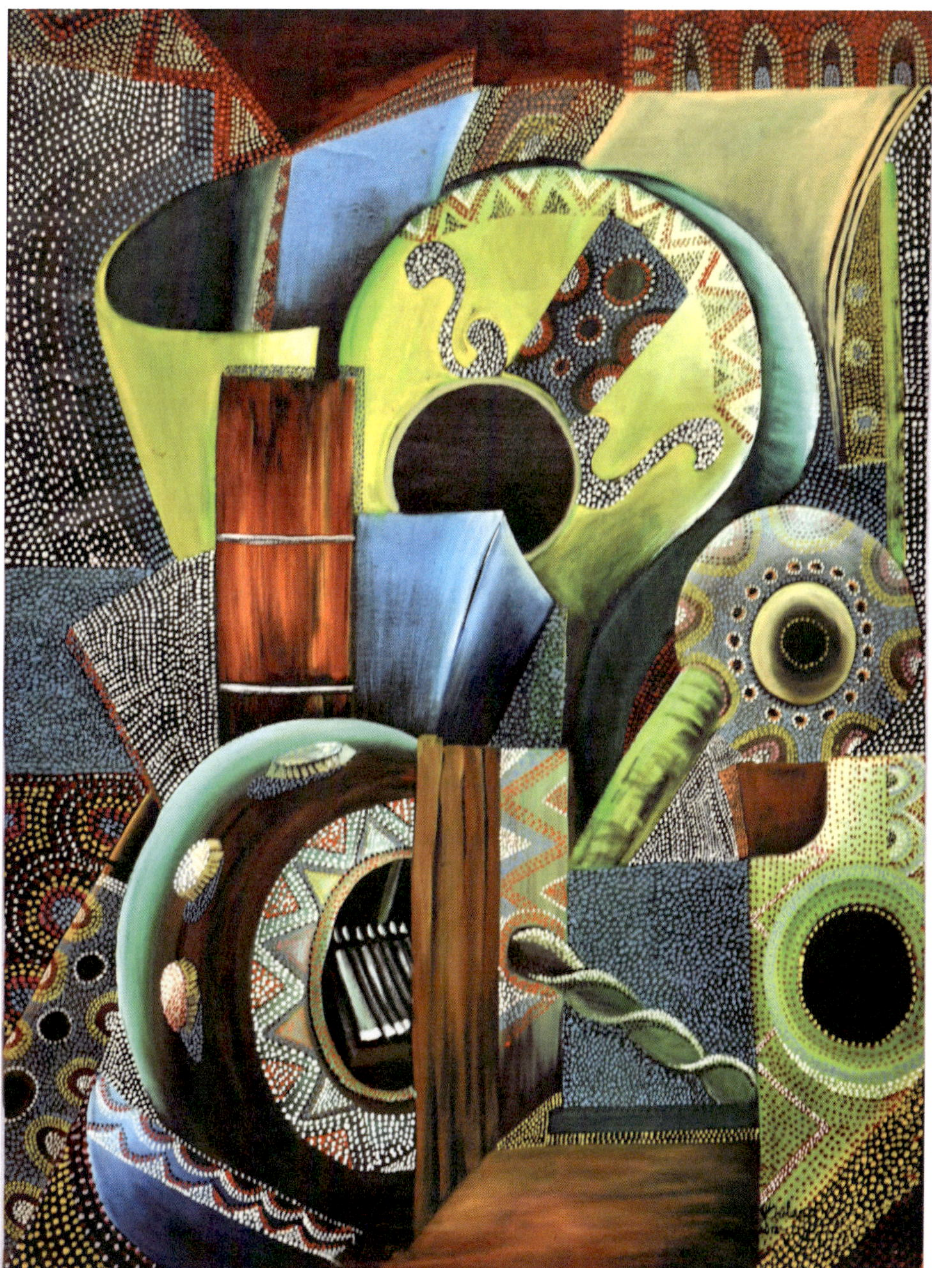

VKM—V002
71 x 99cm

28" x 39"

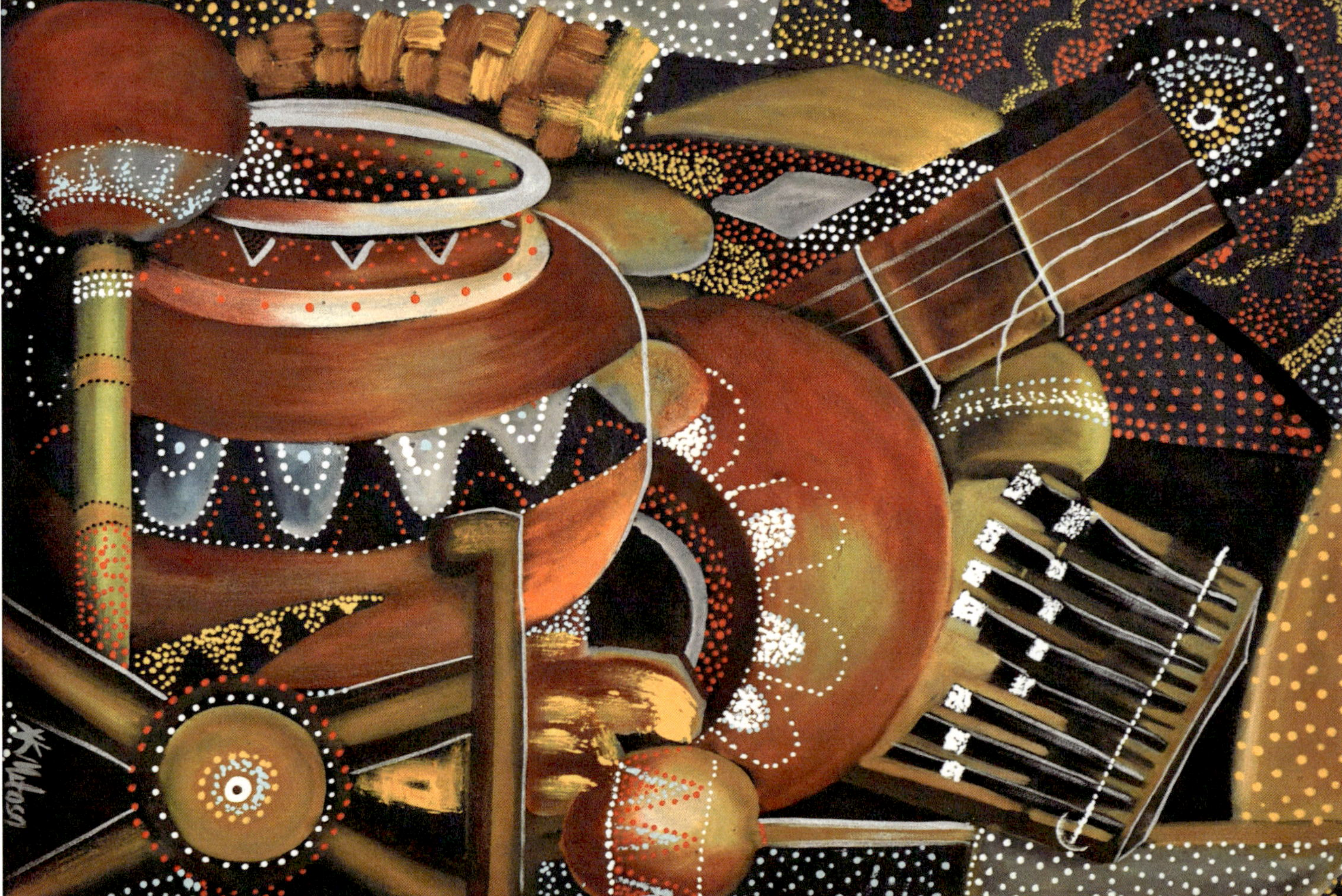

VKM—V003

81 x 58cm

32" x 23"

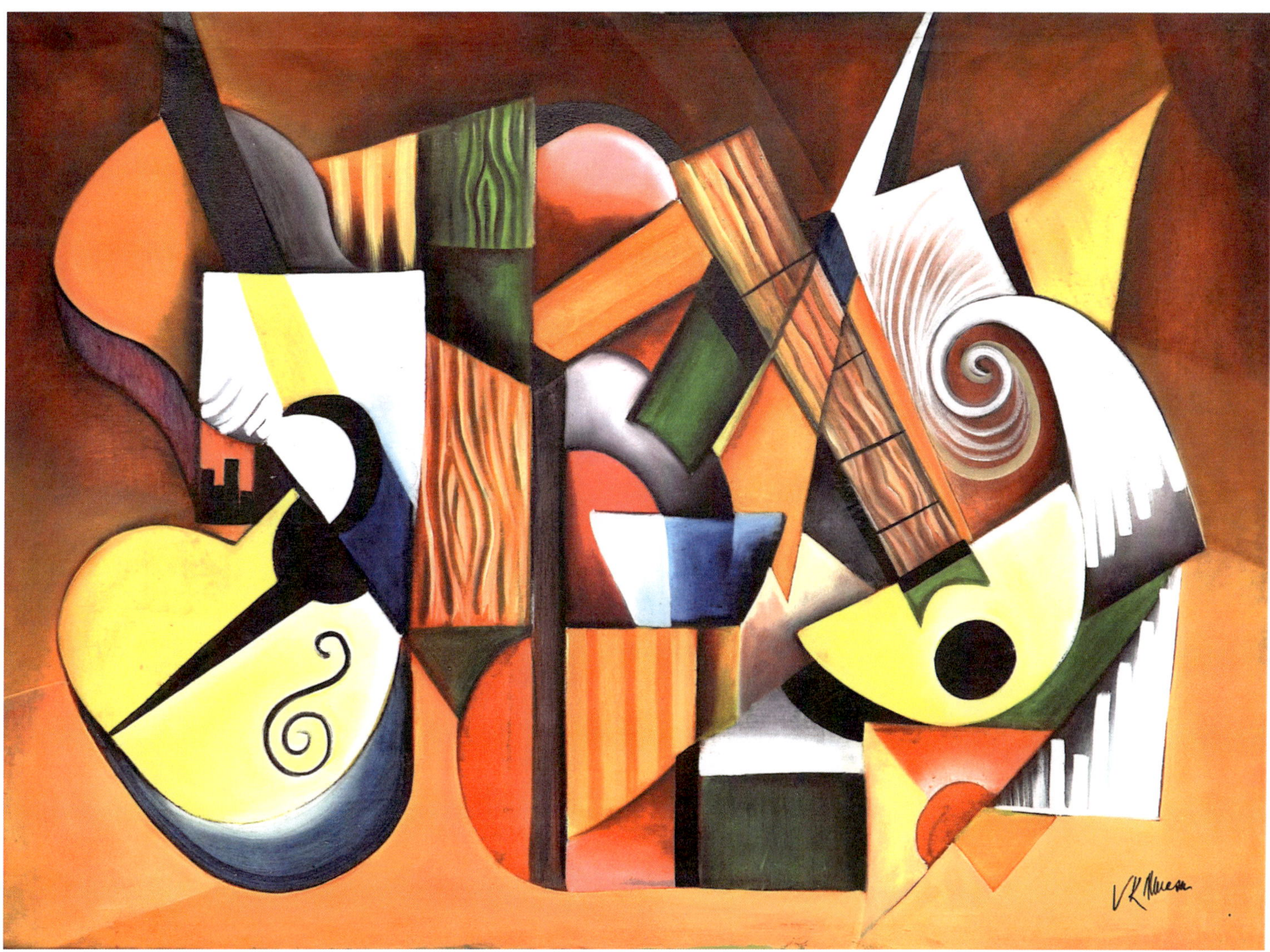

48" x 35"

VKM—V004

123 x 88cm

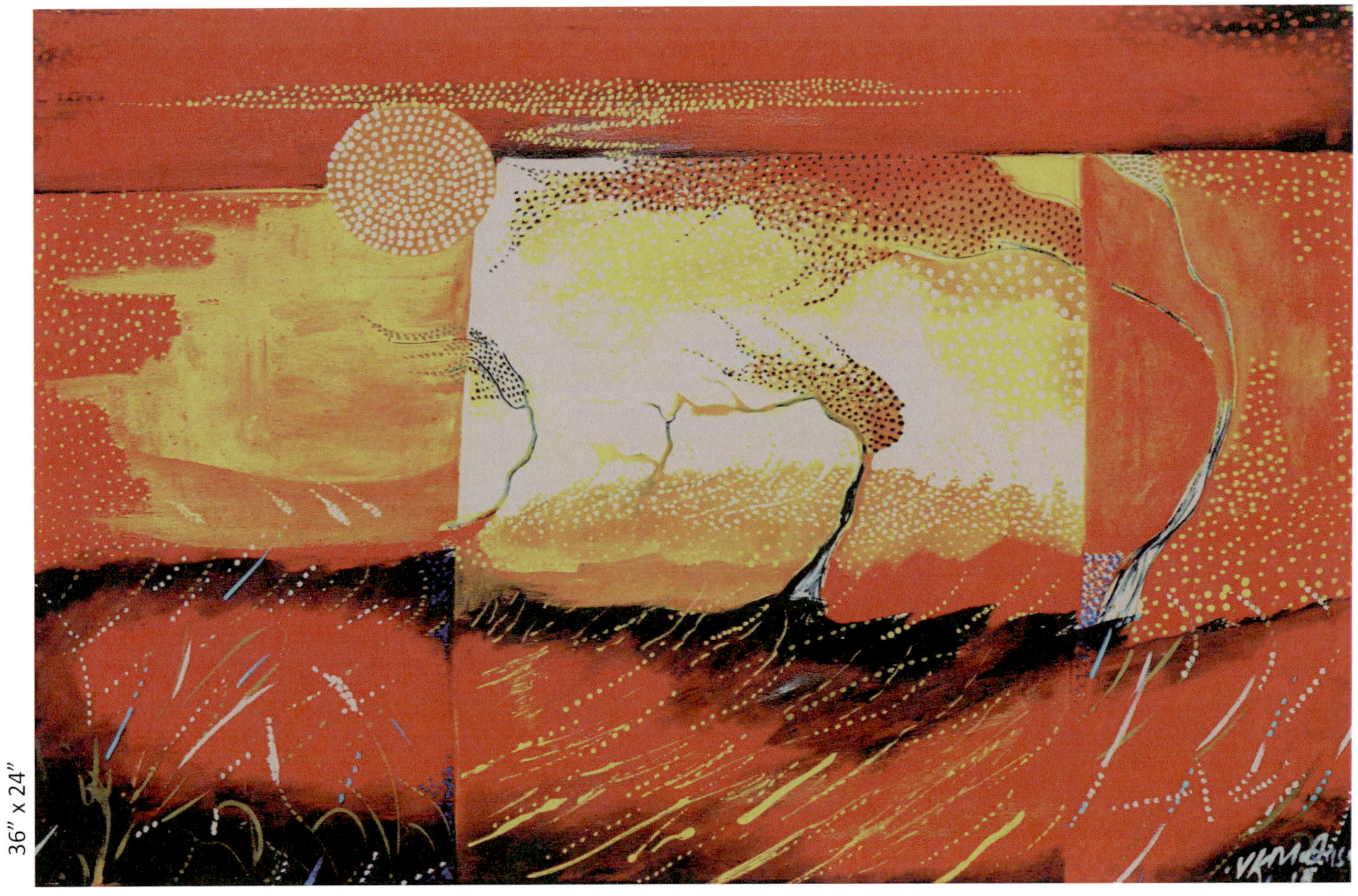

36" x 24"

VKM—V012   91 x 60 cm

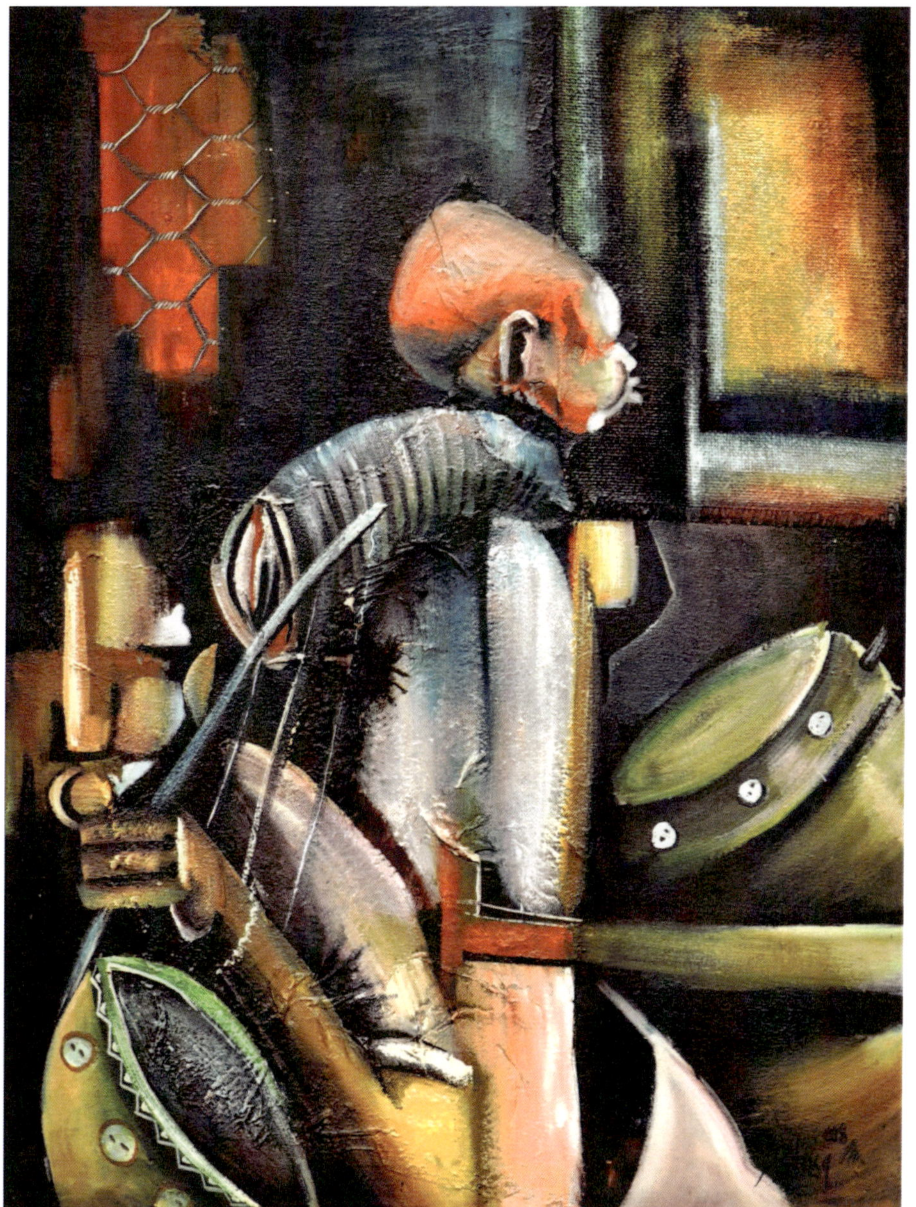

VKM—V006
88 x 123cm

34" x 48"

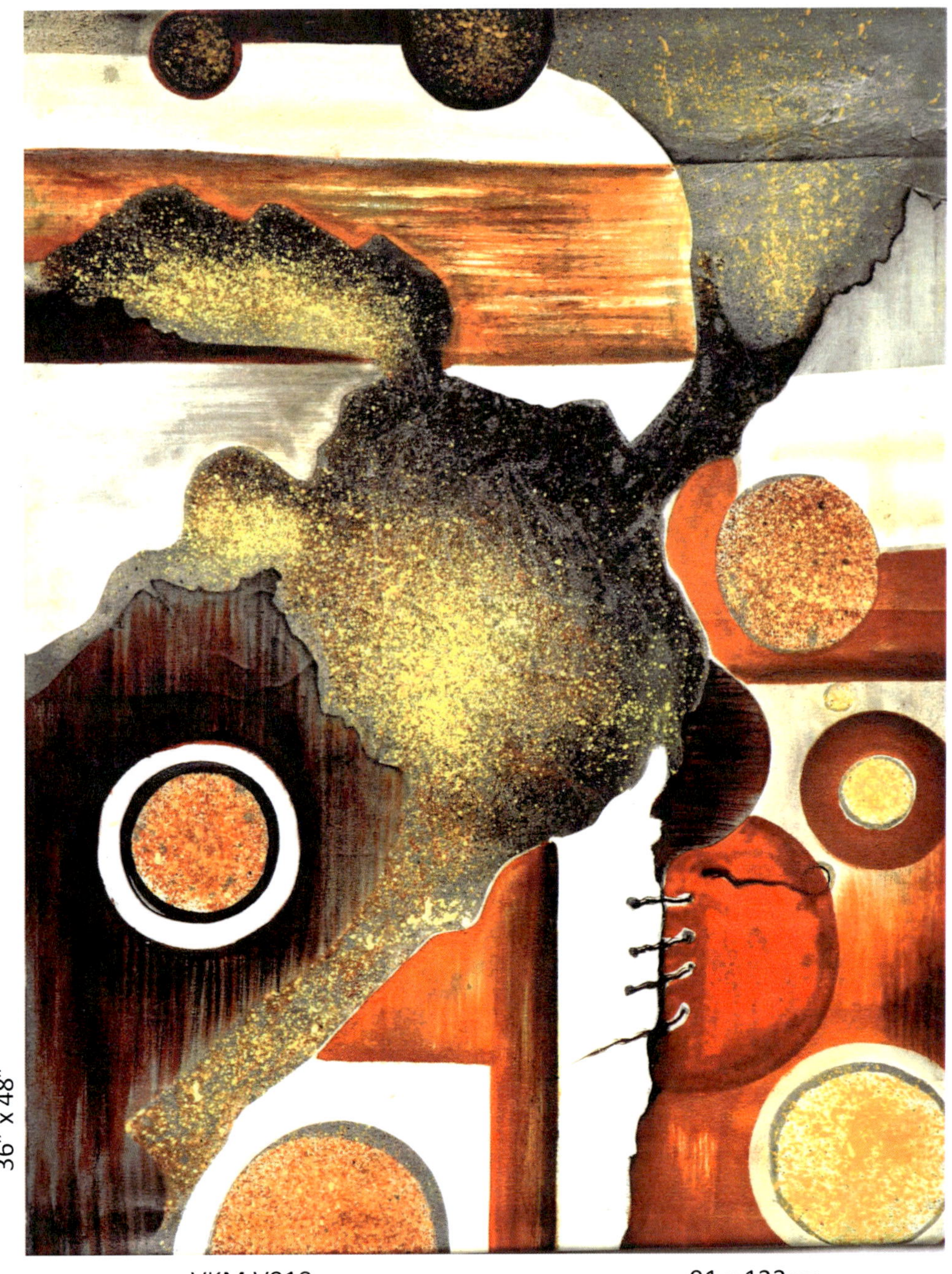

36" x 48"

VKM V010

91 x 123cm

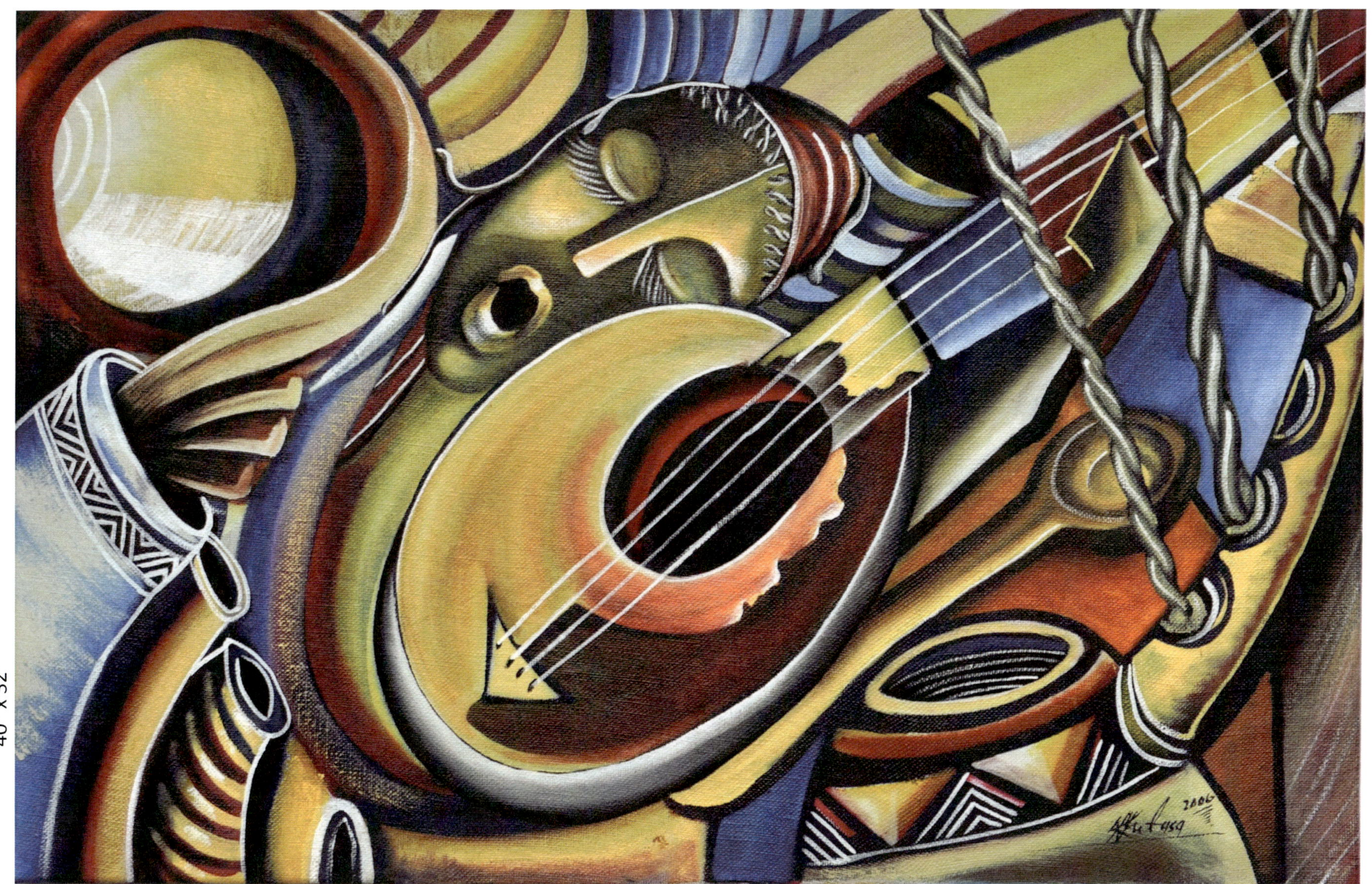

VKM—V001   *The Loudest Noise*   99 x 81cm

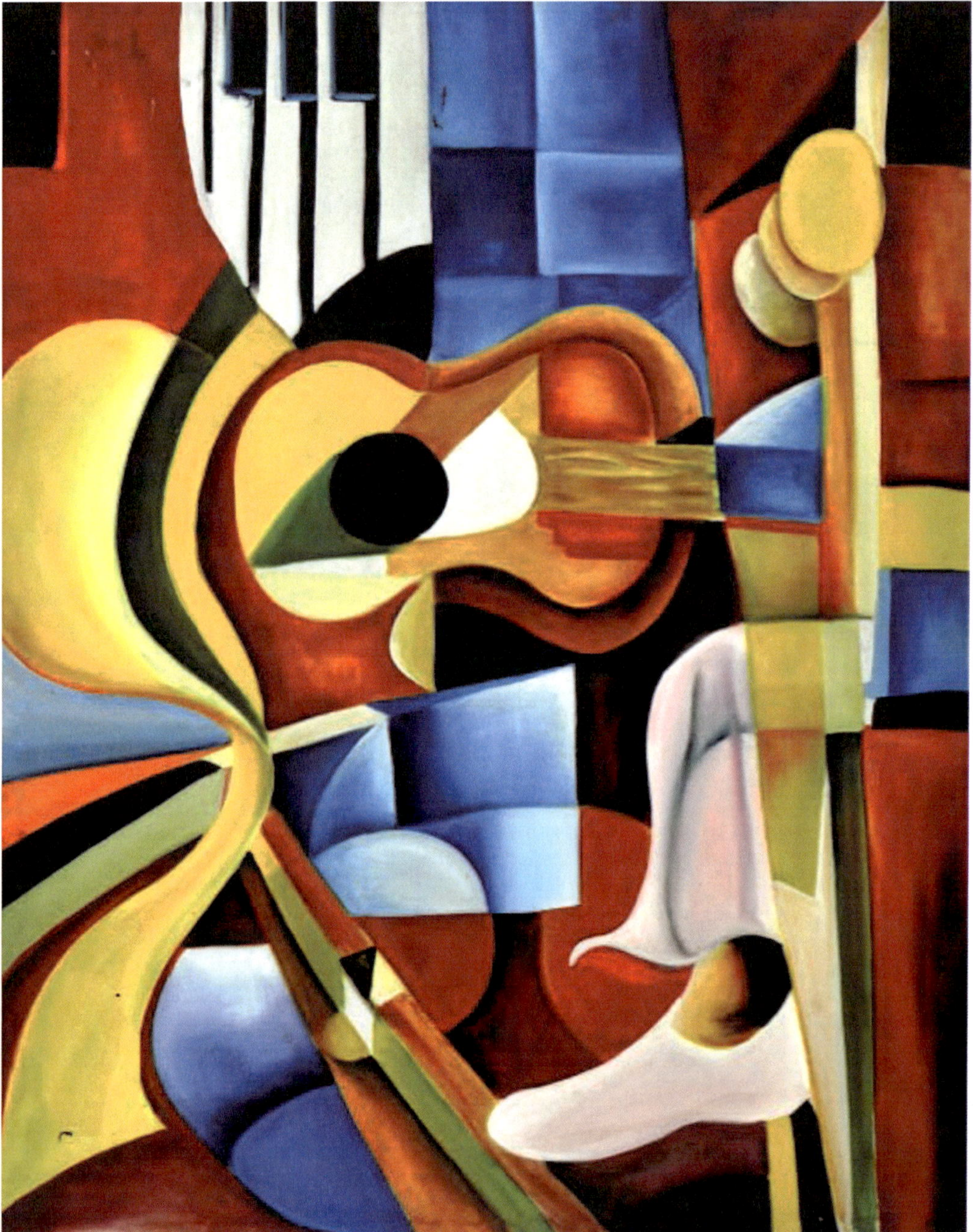

VKM—V009
123 x 91cm

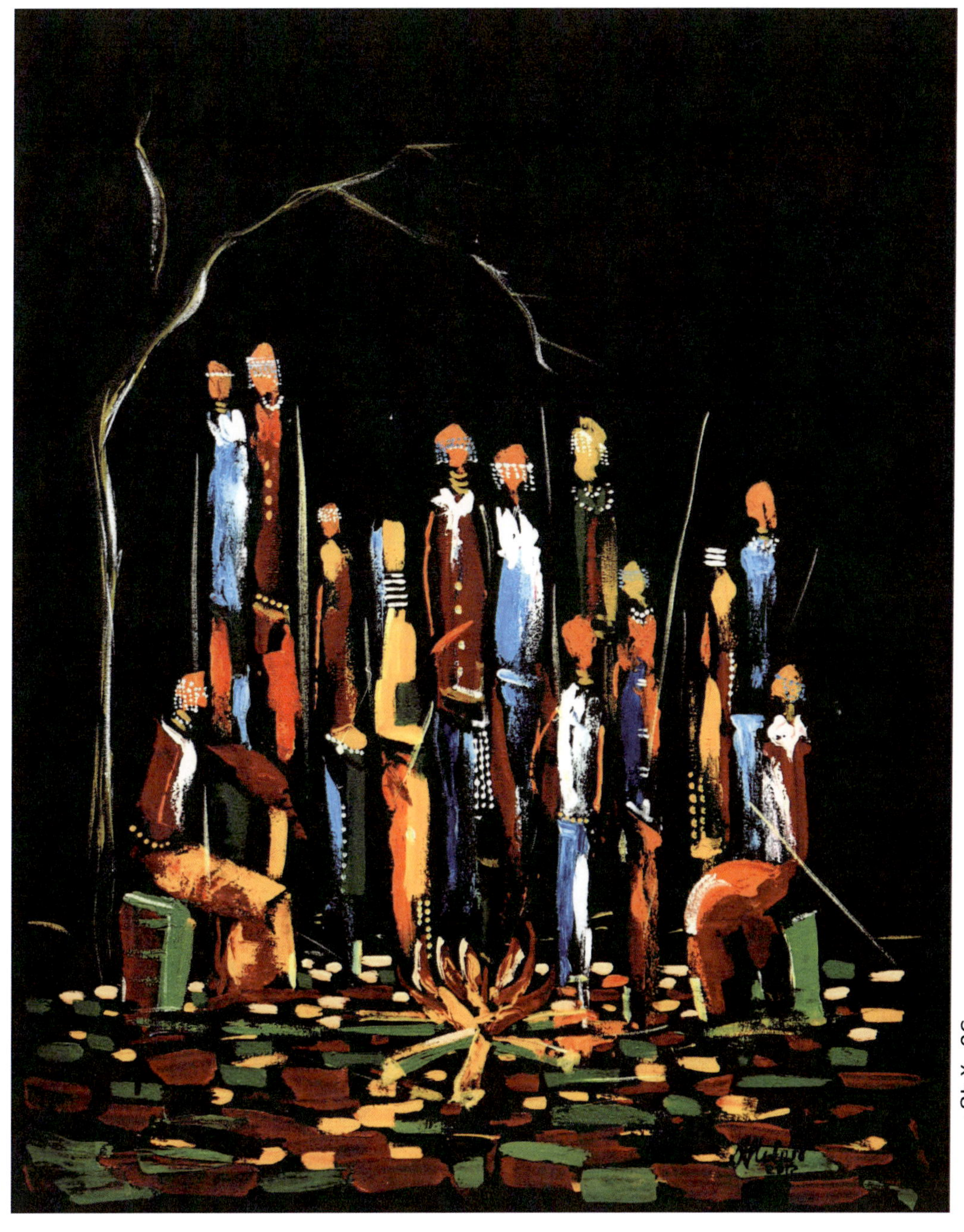

VKM—V008
123 x 91cm
The Gathering

36" x 48"

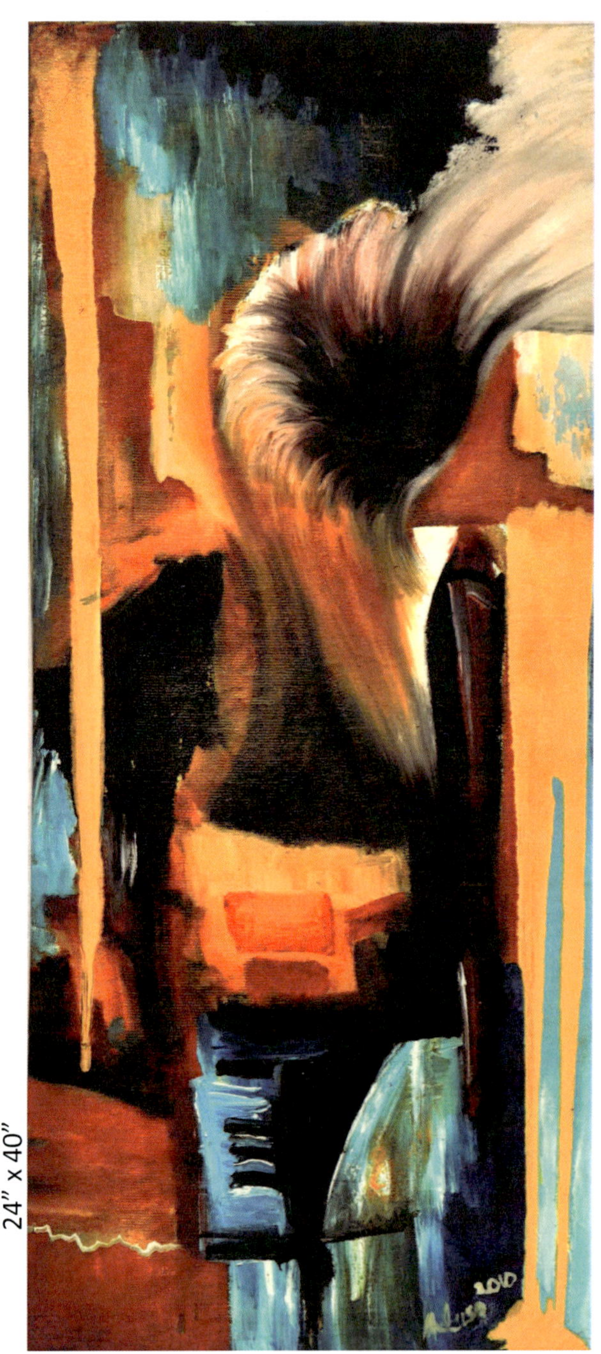

VKM—V016
60 x 102cm

24" x 40"

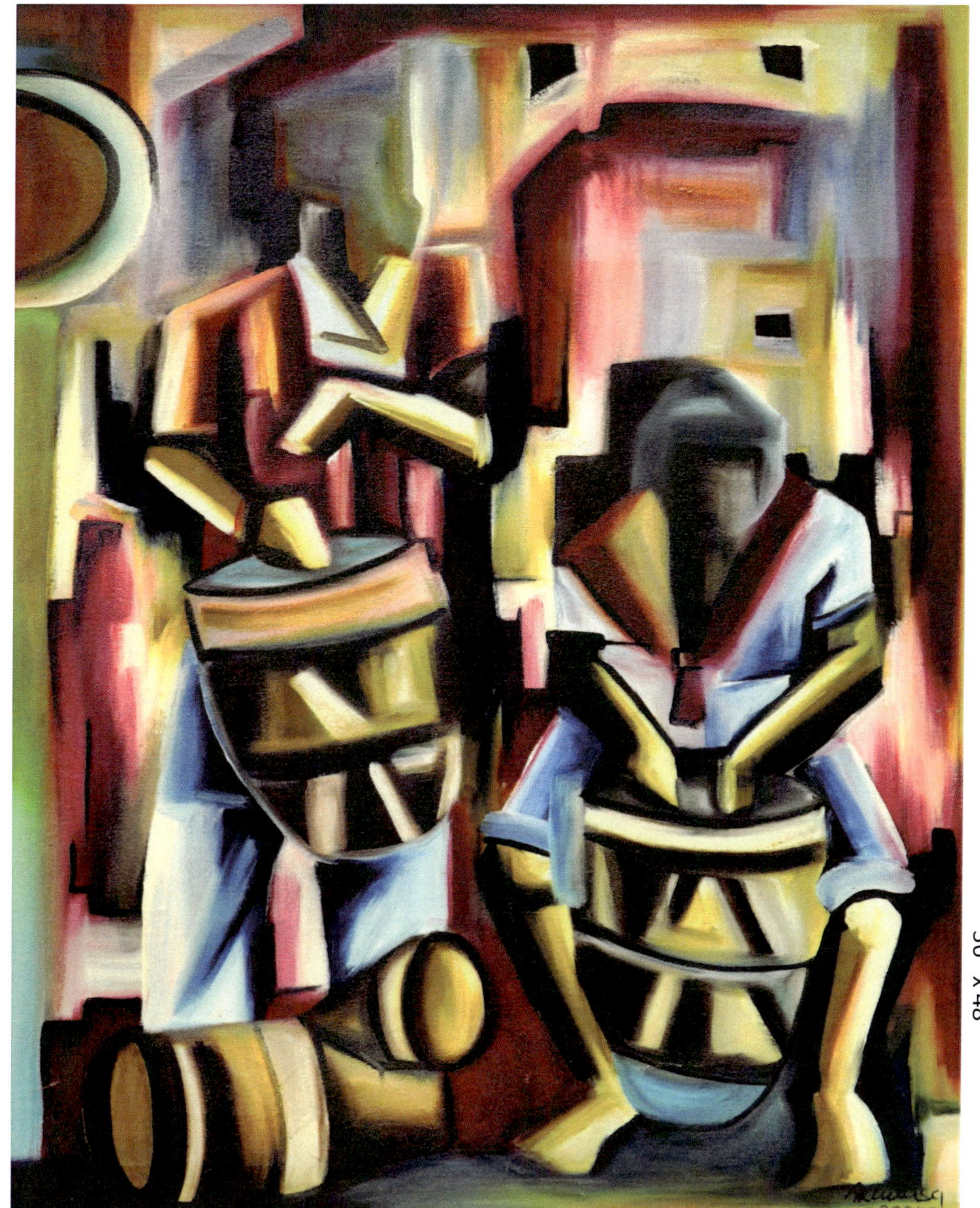

VKM—V015
91 x 123cm

36" x 48"

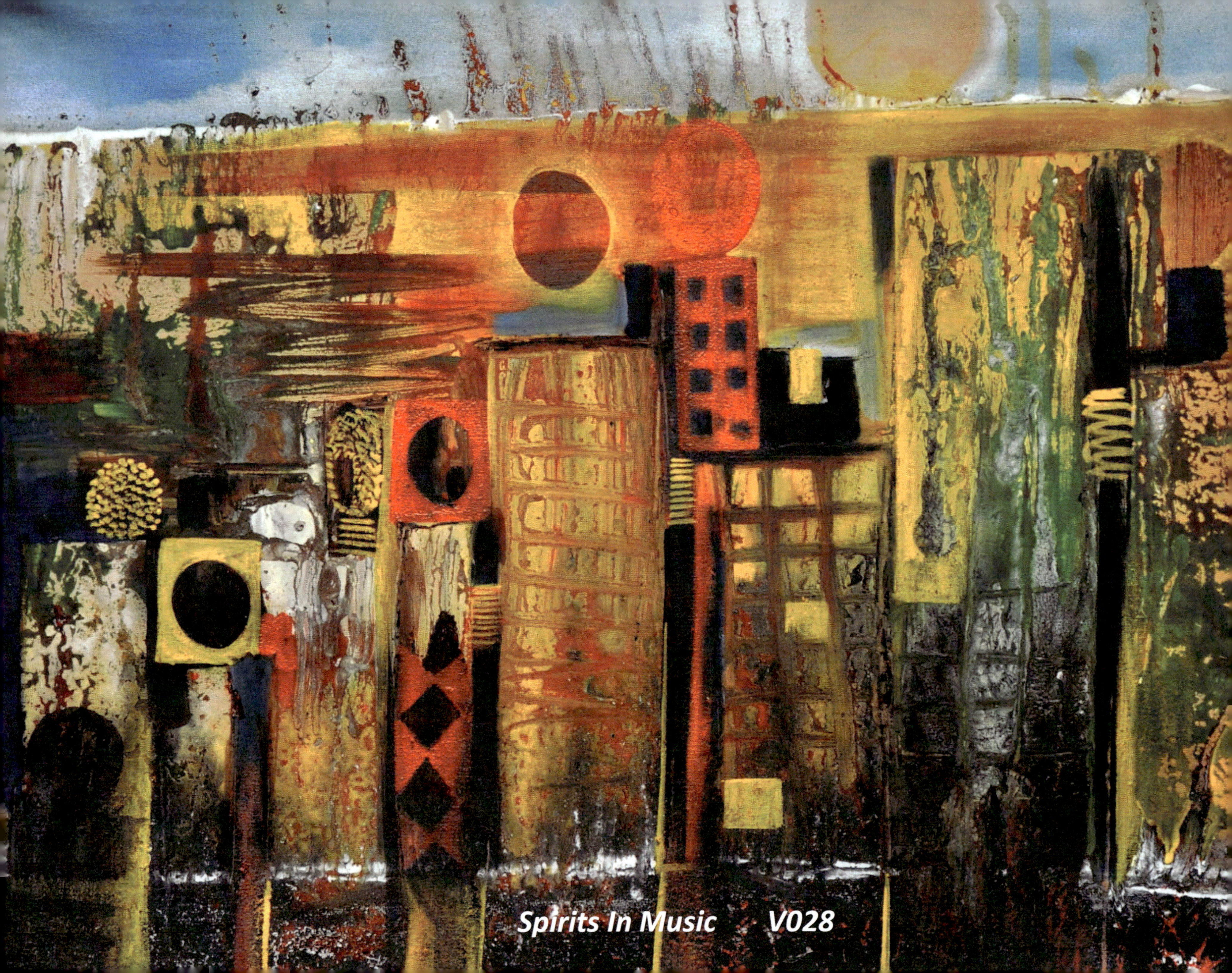

Spirits In Music   V028

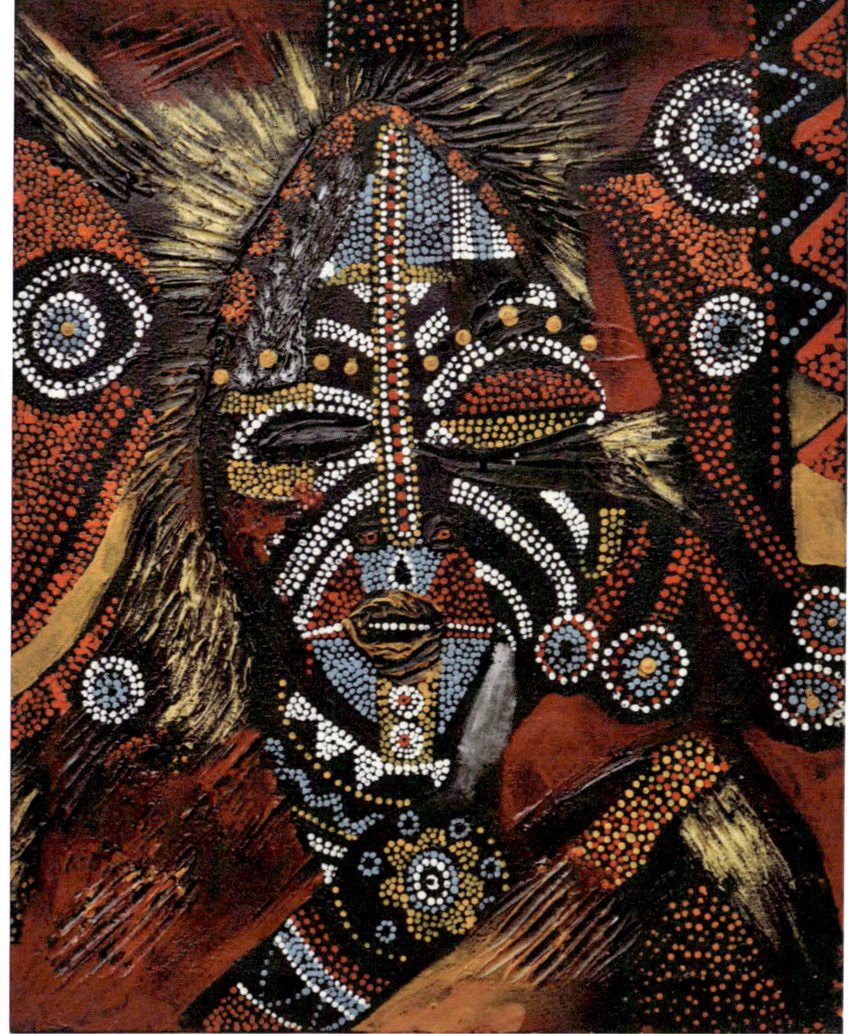

Mixed Media Mask

41 x 51cm
(16 x 20")

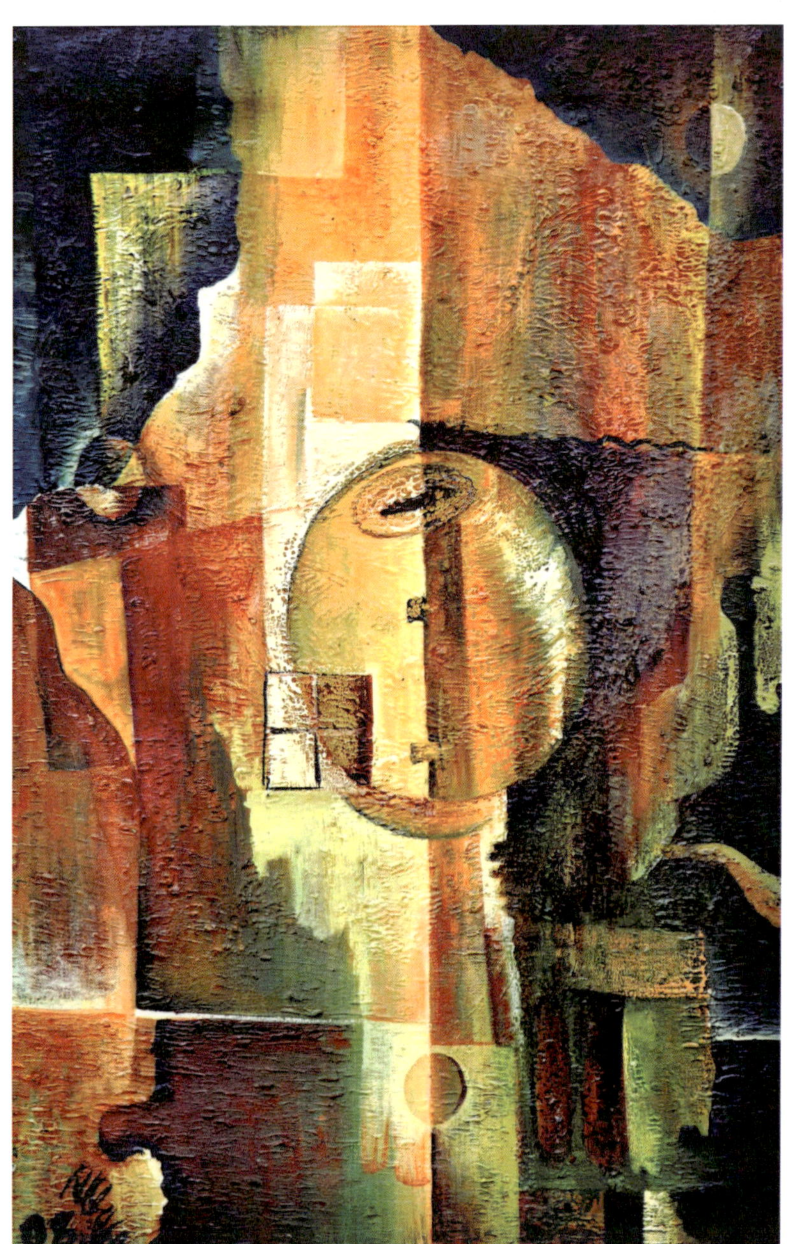

VKM—V035
40 x 60cm

16" x 24"

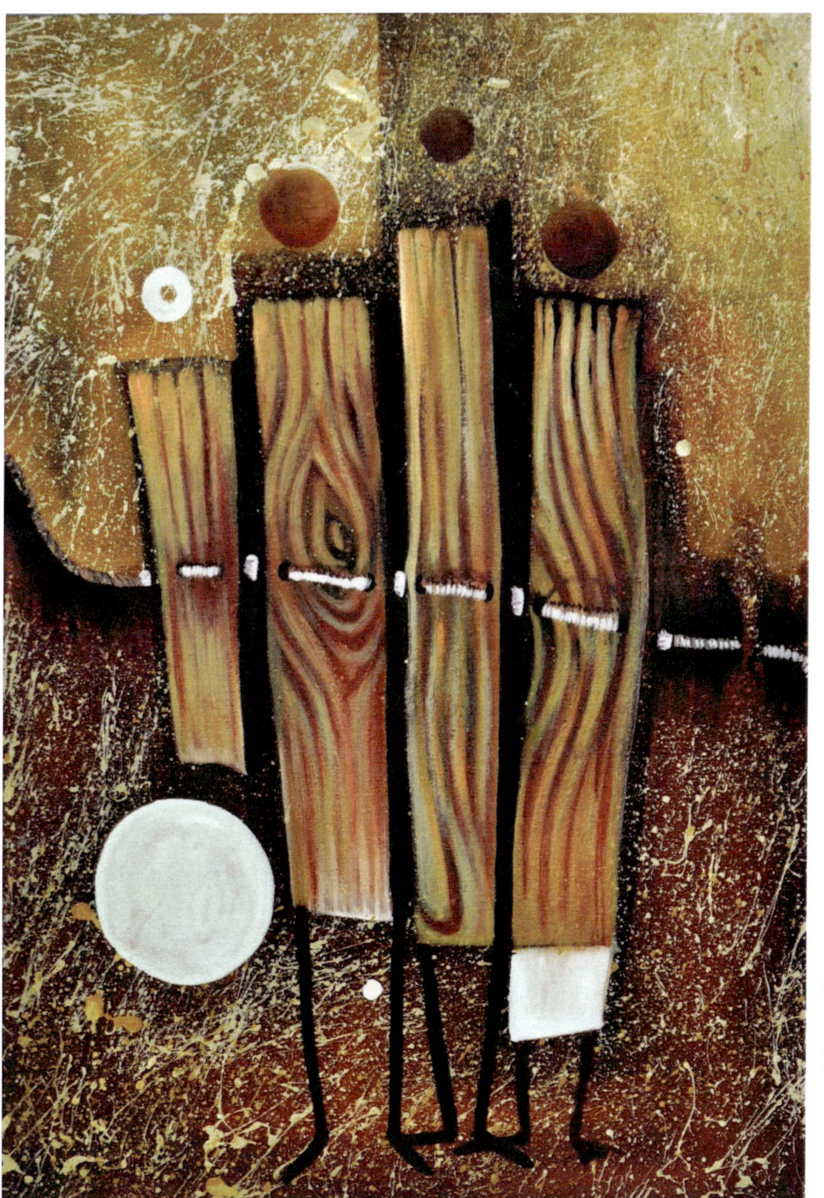

VKM—V041

45 x 60cm

18" x 24"

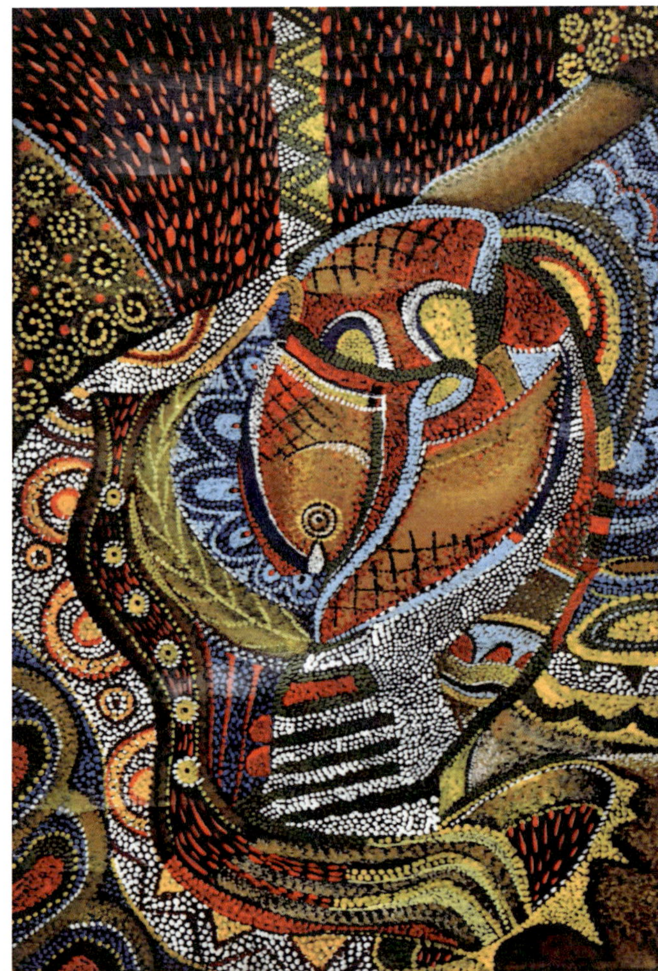

V018   Pointillism Oil On Canvas   40 x 60cm

16" x 24"

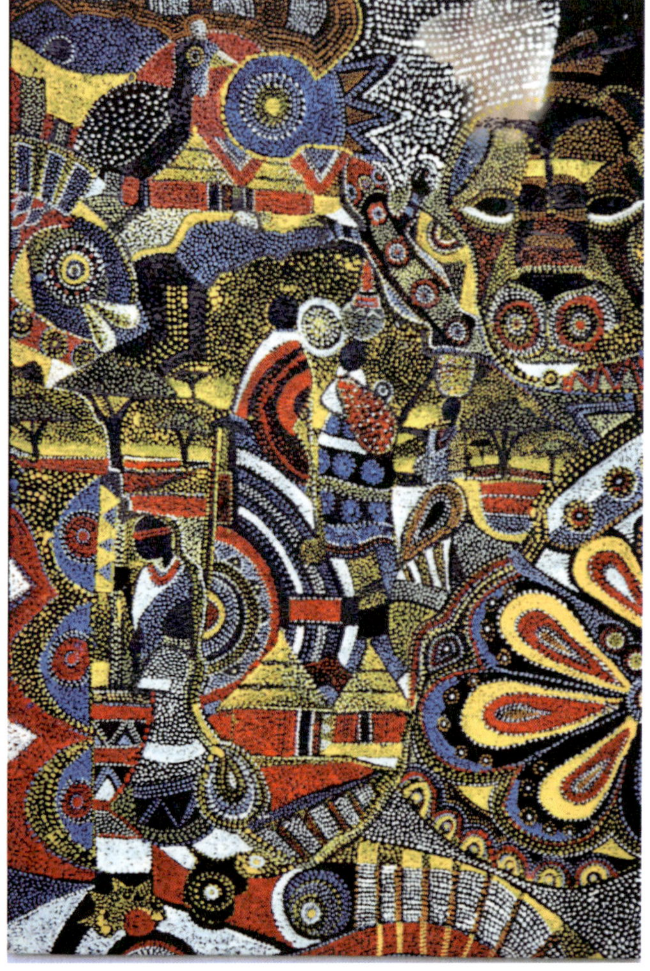

V022   Pointillism Oil On Canvas 40 x 60cm

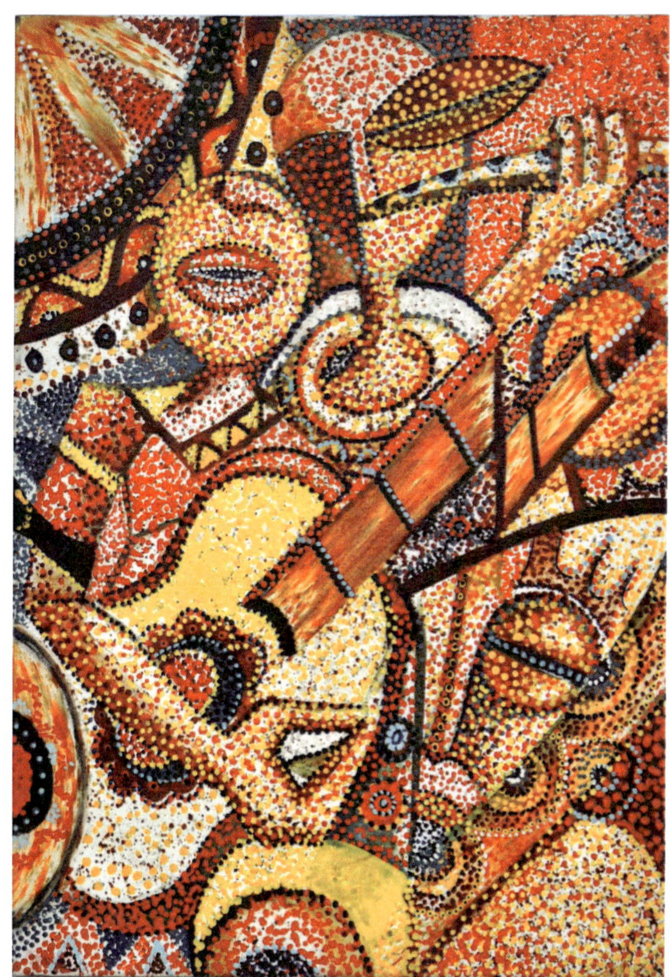

V023   Pointillism Oil On Canvas   40 x 60cm

16" x 24"

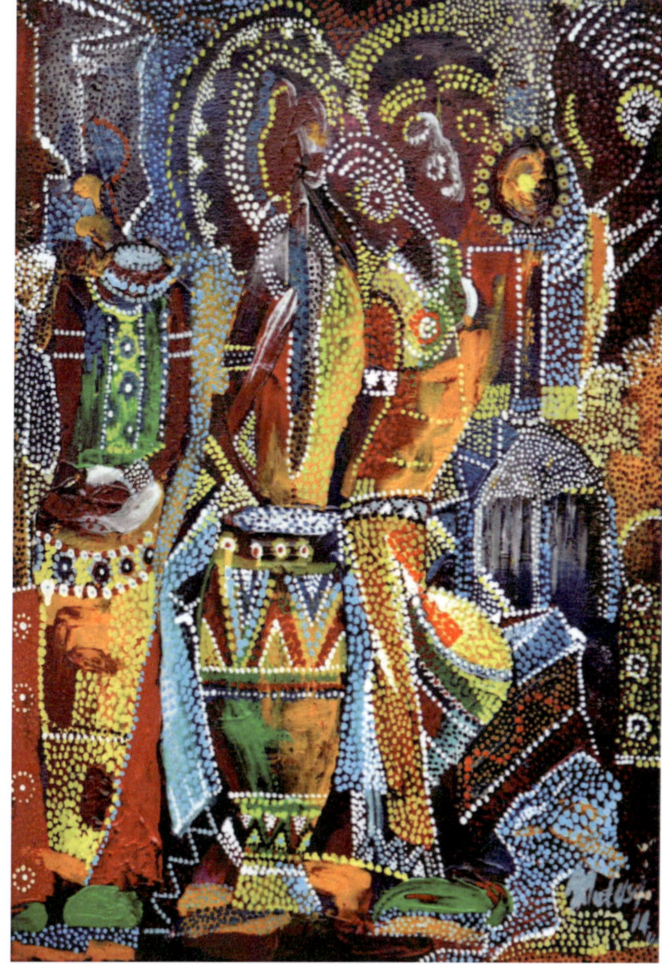

V024   Pointillism Oil On Canvas   40 x 60cm

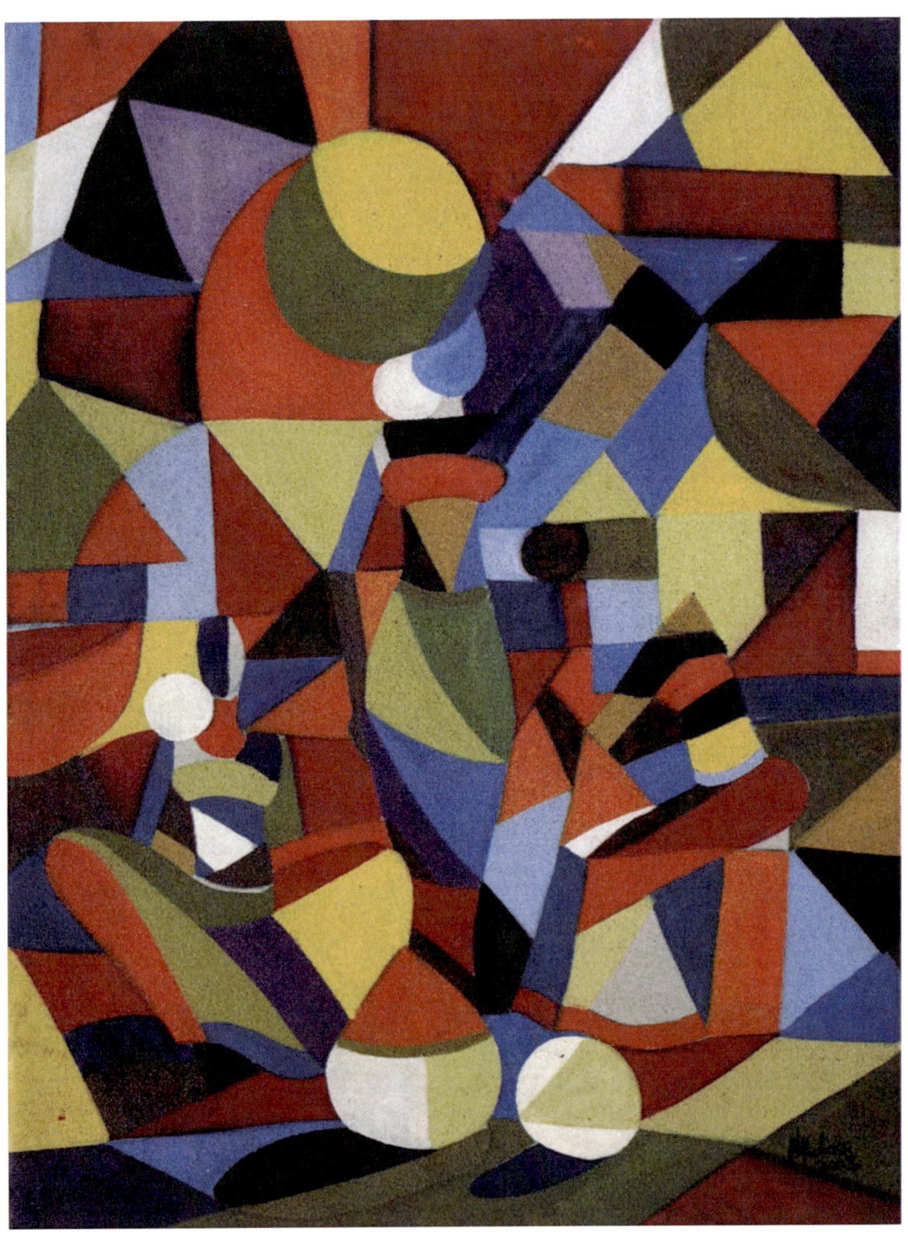

VKM—V090
91 x 123cm
36" x 48"

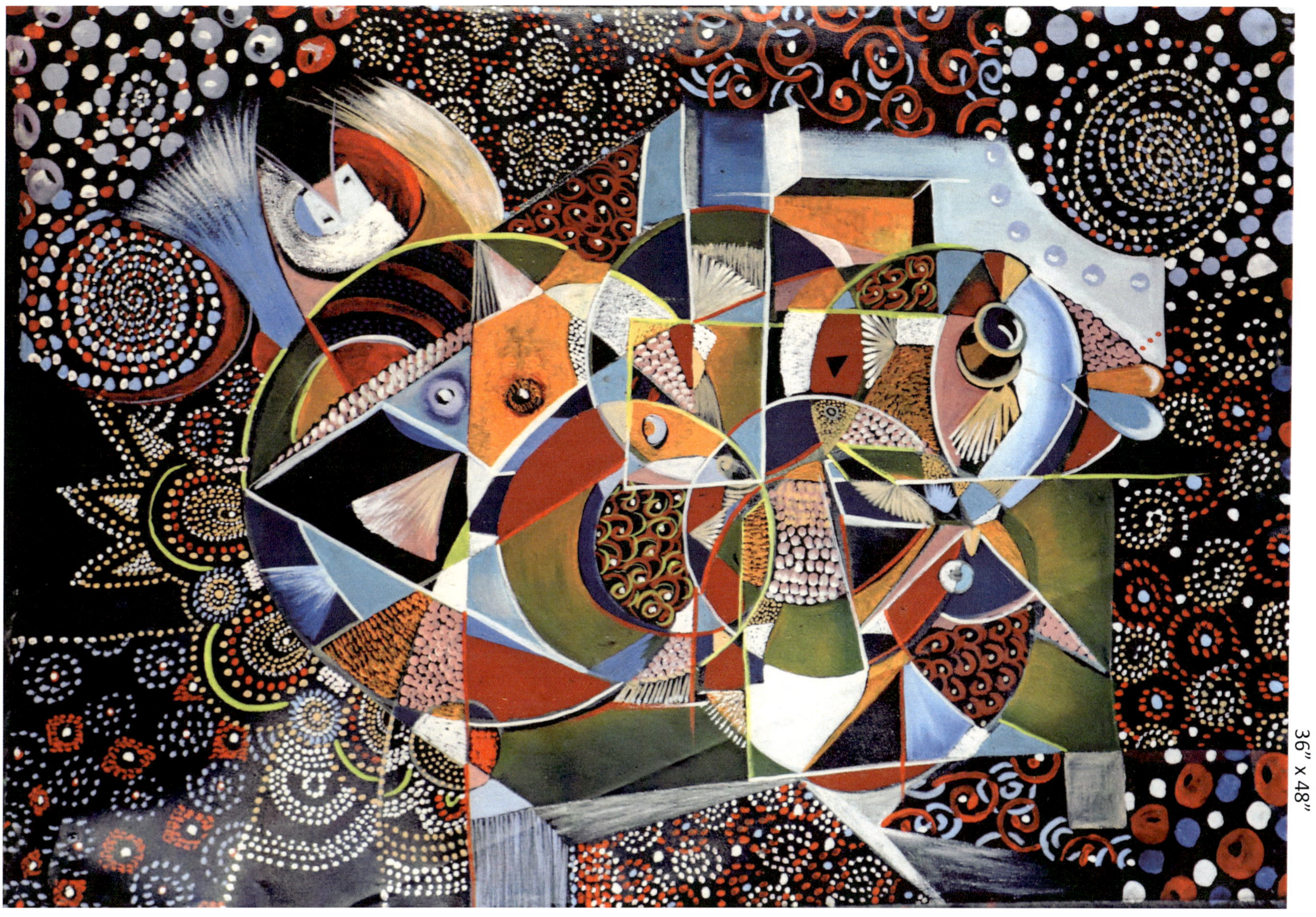

VKM—V20219

36" x 48"

123 x 91cm

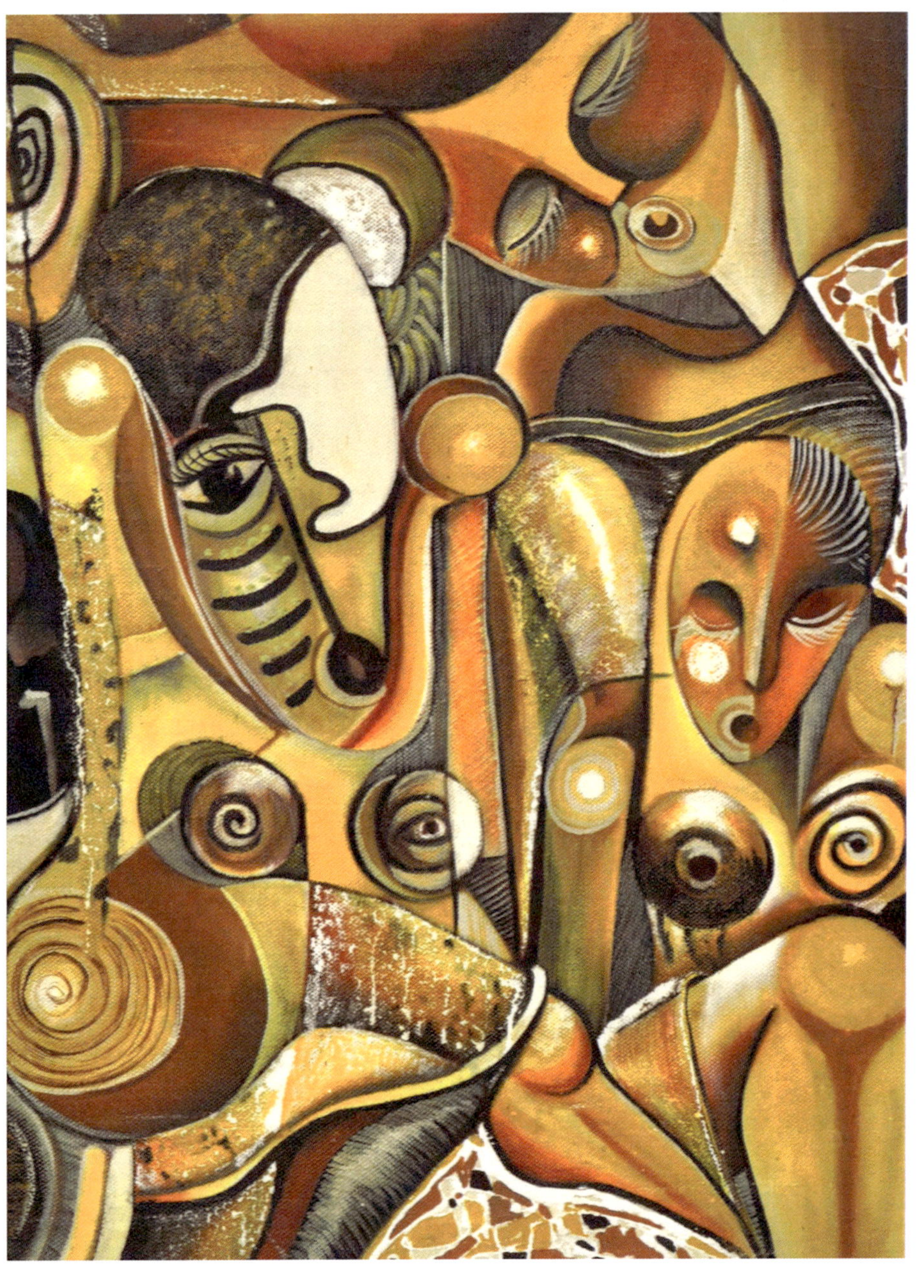

VKM—V062
91 x 123cm

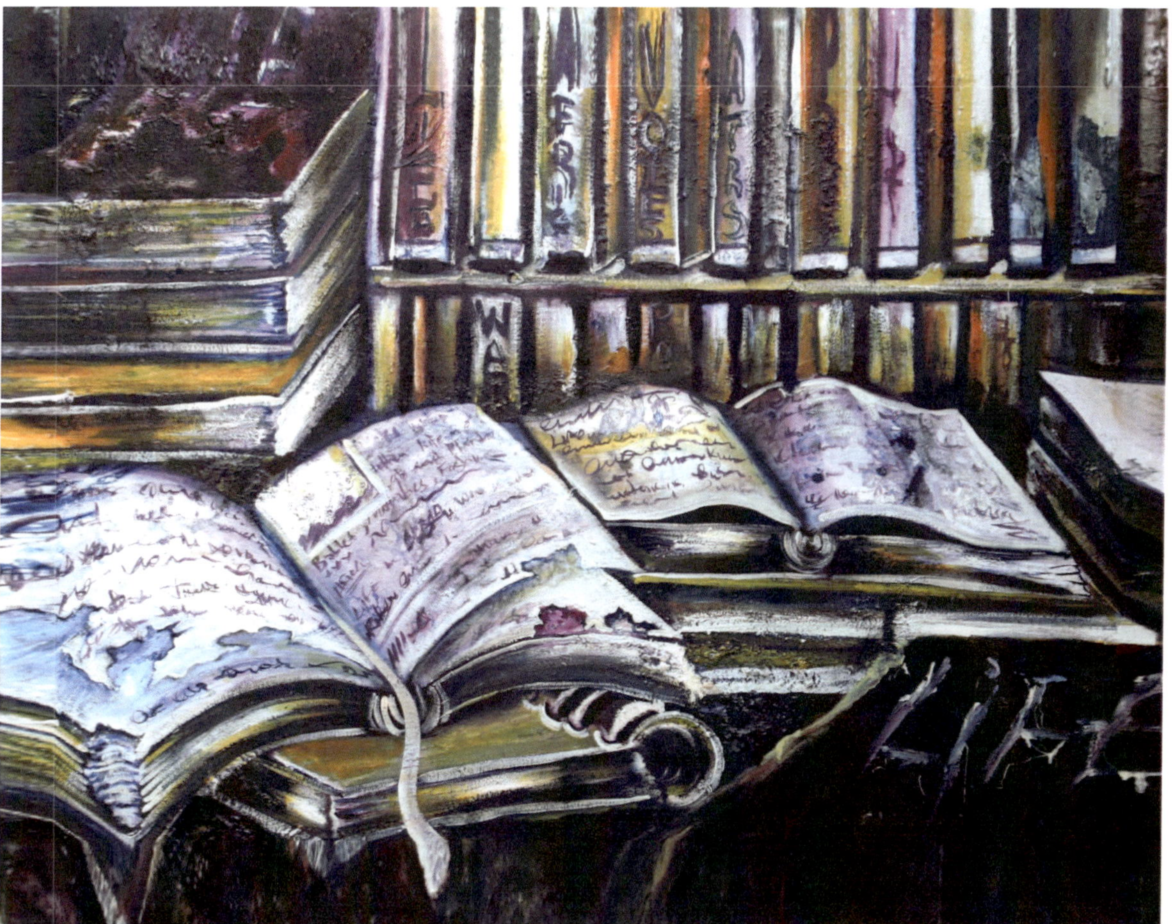

18" x 26"

V095   45 x 66cm

30" x 42"

VKM—V125   106 x 76cm

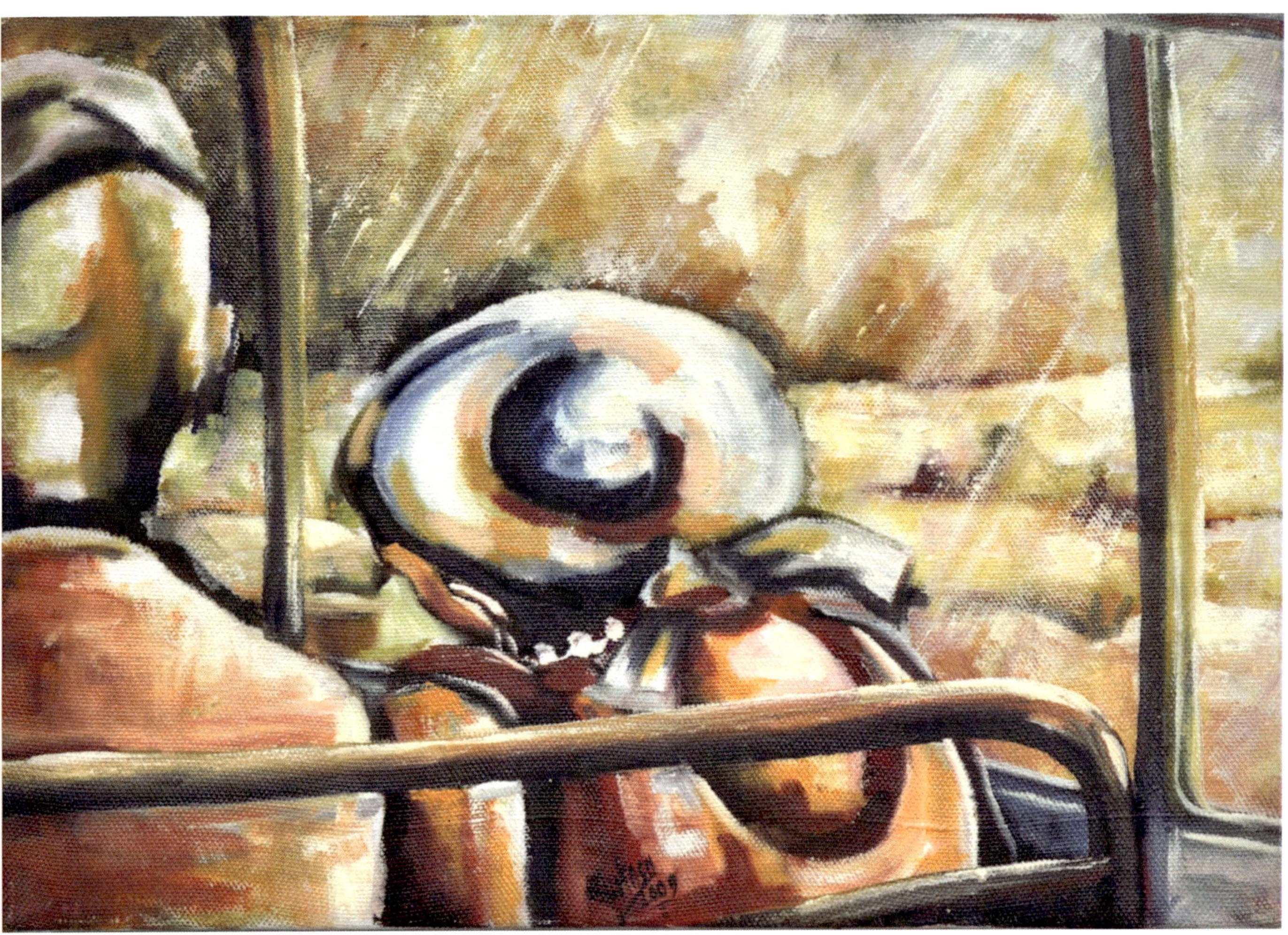

Bus Trip In The Rain　　　　　　V051

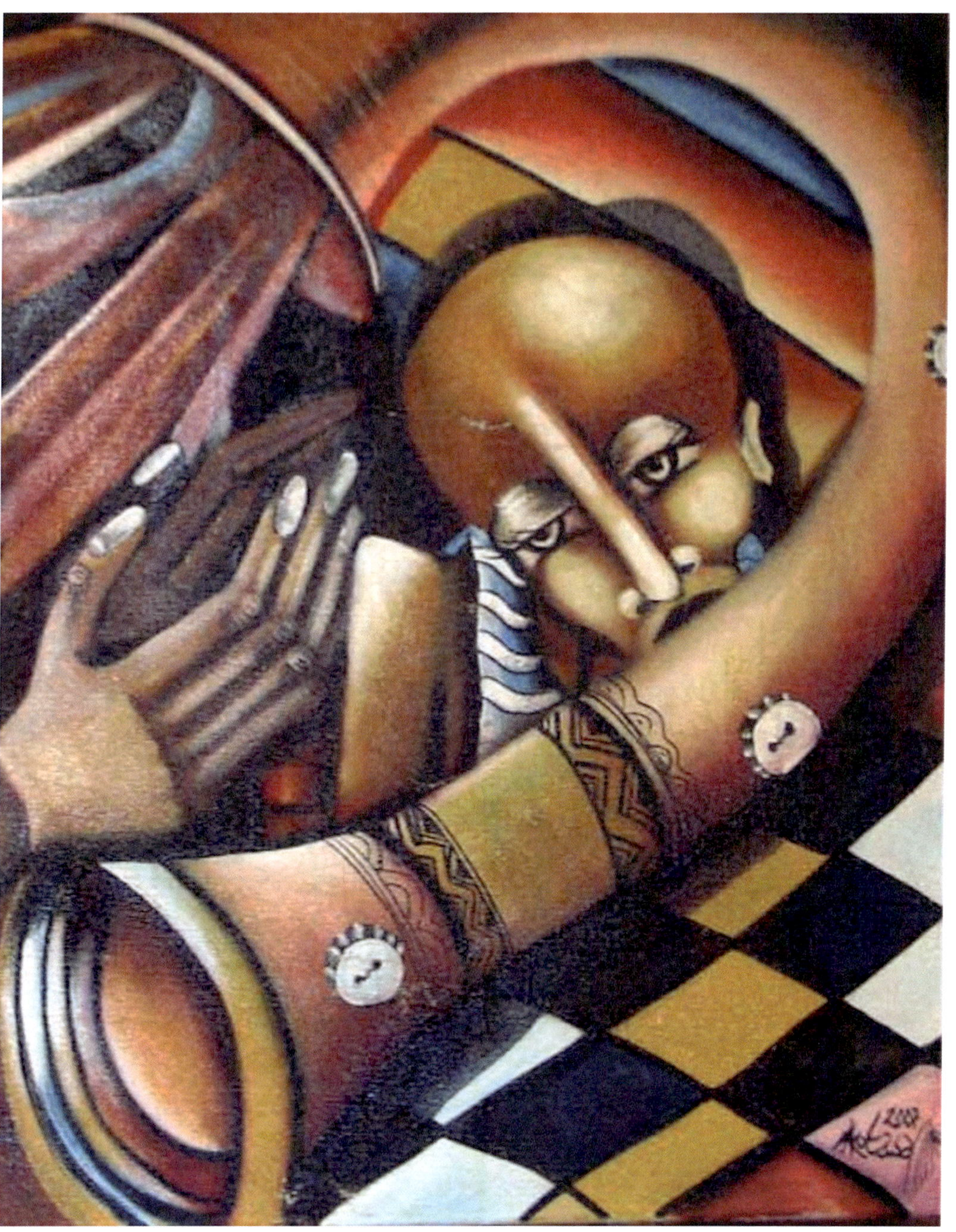

V051

28" x 30"

71 x 76cm

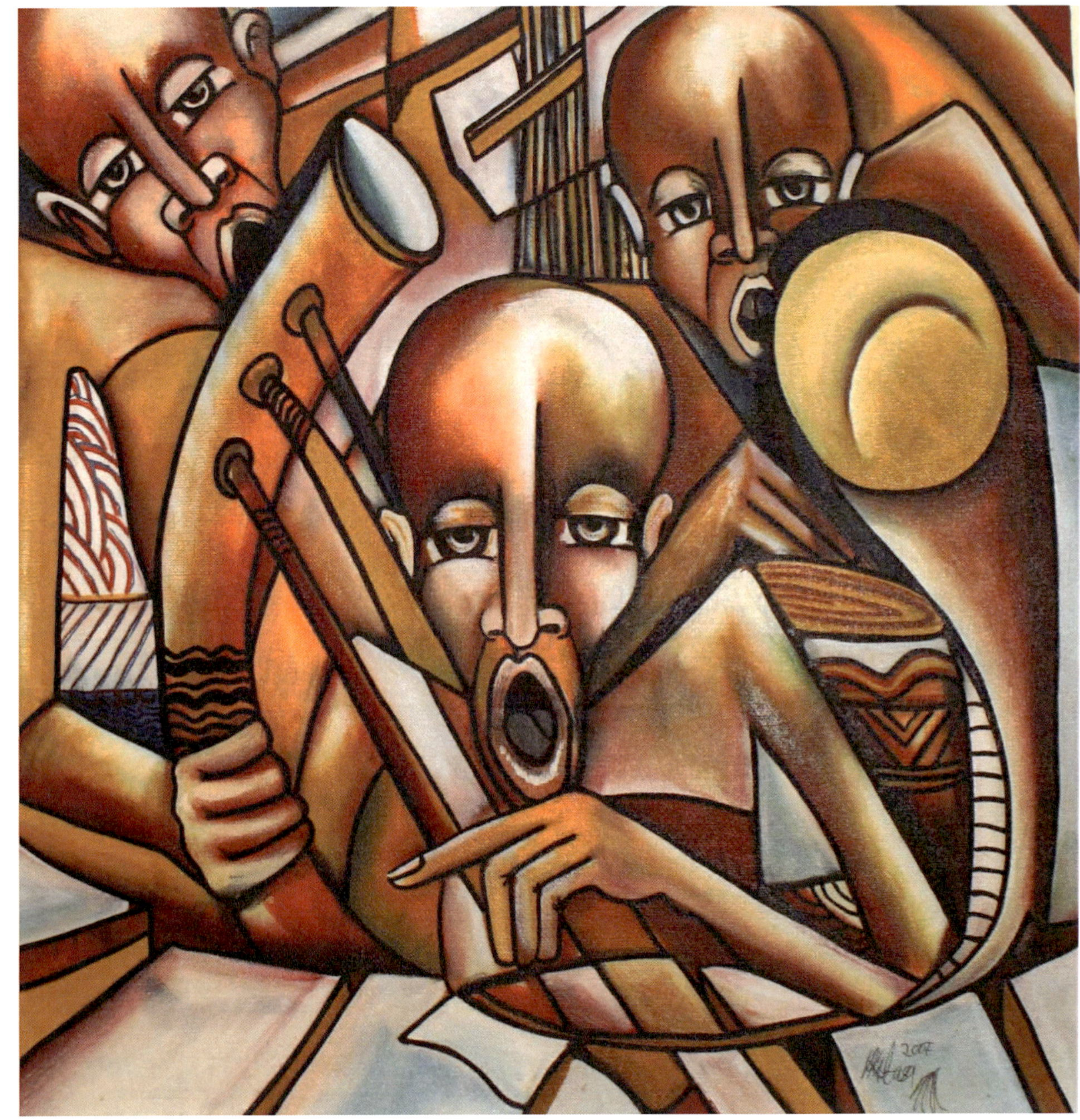

V108
76 x 76cm
(30" x 30")

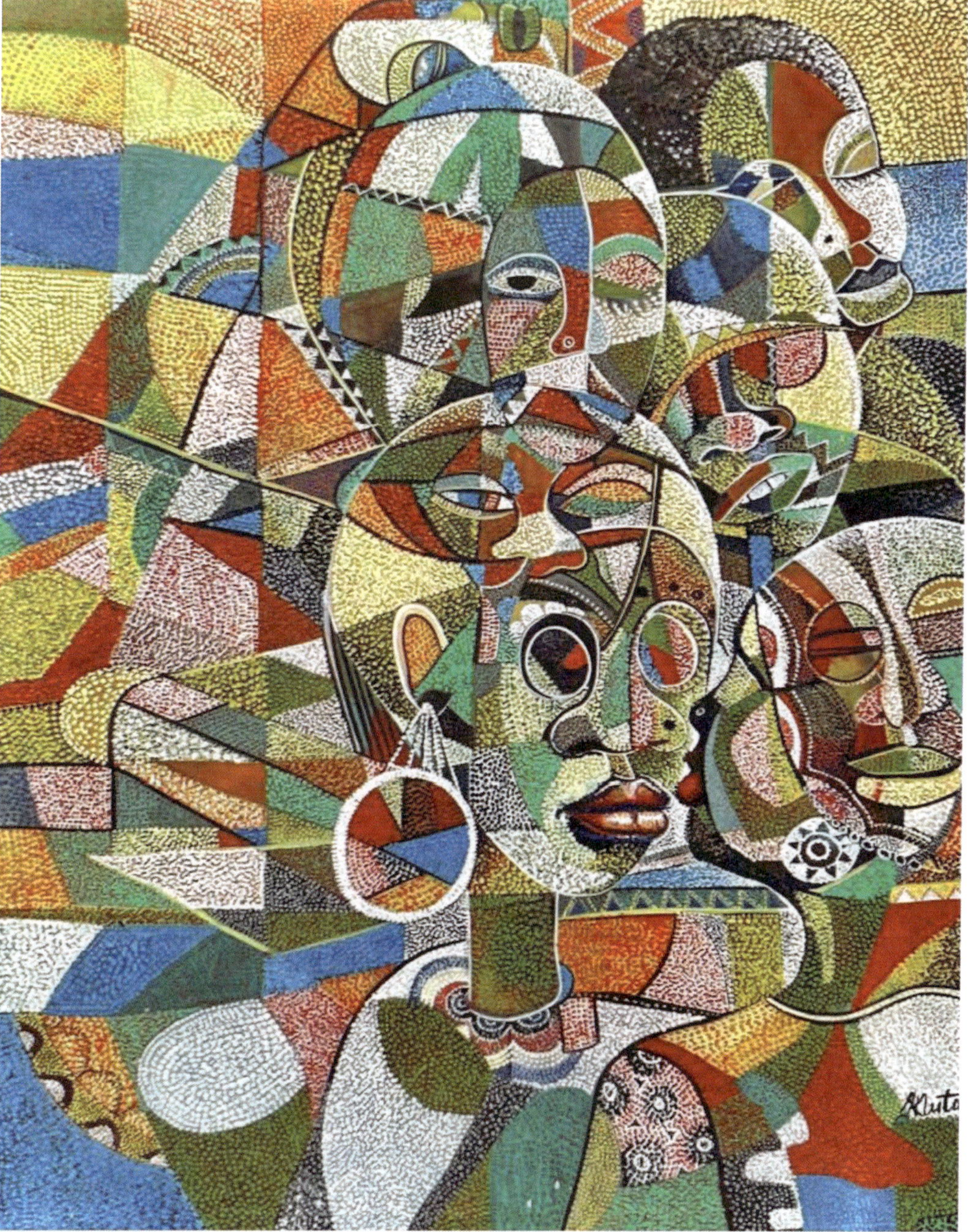

V202322
Pointillism Oil On Canvas
91 x 123cm
(36" x 48")

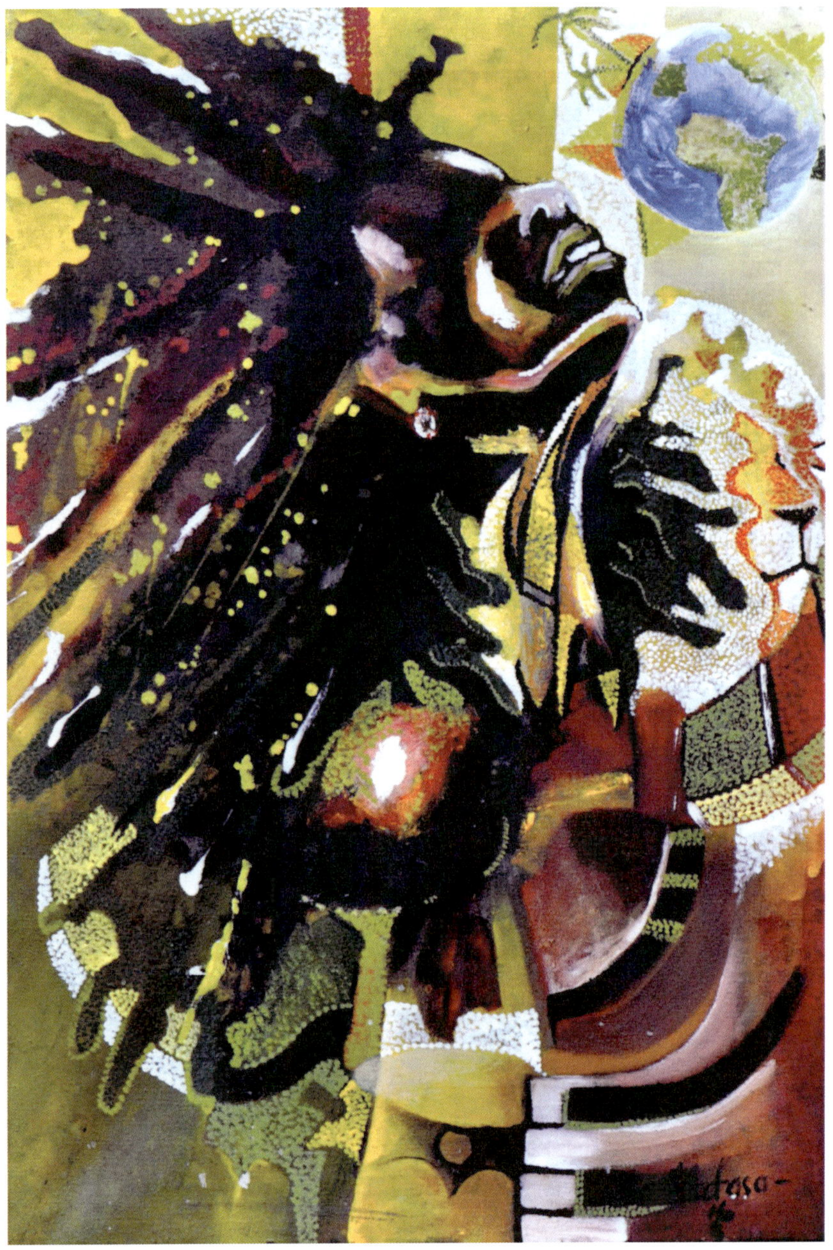

V088
33 x 48cm

(continued from p6) enterprise. Obviously, the law of supply and demand was at play, the tourists who came from the USA and Europe to Zimbabwe looked for that kind of African imagery and these boys were there to meet the demand. Unconfident of why and what it was that had brought me here with such urgency, I just stood around trying hard to give the impression of a potential big order buyer. The older boys who were not involved in the actual painting turned out to be runners who delivered the finished product to their vendors in the city center. I composed myself and made small talk with them. I knew I was not buying anymore but neither did I feel like giving any of them a lecture on the "ramifications of negative depictions of Africans in art", it was not the time or the place for it. So while my vendor/guide was haggling with a young man he was calling "Sizza" (Ceasar), the obvious head of the operation, over price to purchase more canvasses to replenish his stocks which I had depleted: I walked around looking at the work of the boys in the "committees" painting heads, torso and skinny legs in the assembly line.

a tree in the yard to dry. The same young man was also drawing the outlines of the figures to be painted on by the rest of the committees. I drifted towards his station and struck a conversation with him.

Unlike everyone else that I had observed in the group, he was not cracking jokes. He seemed oblivious to the chatter around him. Unlike the painters with brushes and buckets of the one black color paint, he had an array of paint tubes scattered around him. He was concentrating on his work, mixing the colors, creating the backgrounds for the black figures the rest of the young men would paint on. As I hovered over him, I asked his name. He looked up with an easy smile and said Valentine. I asked him a few non- intrusive questions about their operation to which he responded confidently with a disarming charm. Emboldened by his forthright answers, I asked him why, with his obvious talent, they were producing artworks of ugly caricatures of Africans. "Its just business boss, that's what the tourists buy. That's what sells fast." I had no rejoinder to that logic, especially to impoverished youth trying to make an honest living. "So is this, all you do?" "No boss. I do my other painting at home." "Where is home?" "Here in Newlines, not far from not far from here." "Can we go there so I can see, what you do? "Without hesitation, Valentine stood up. He was a tall skinny young man with broad shoulders and a smile that came naturally to his face. As he followed me to my car, he called out to Sizza. "I am going home. I will be right back." Sizza shrugged his shoulders and said "OK" but I thought I saw a hint of disapproval on h i s f a c e .

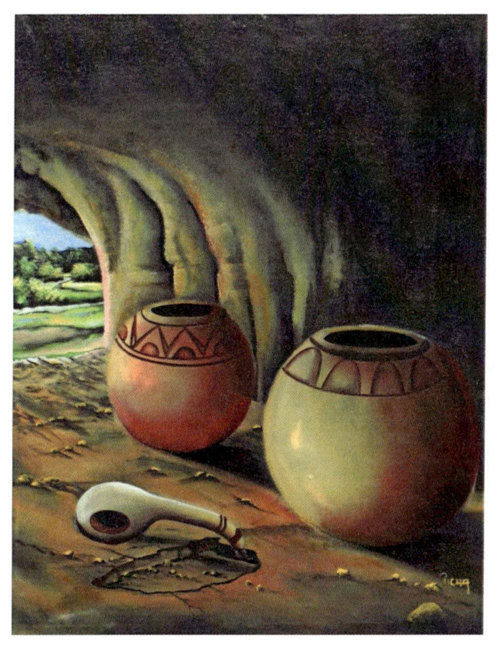

In the banter that was going on among the boys I heard either the word or the name "picasso" but it did not mean anything to me then because a word with so many vowels can mean anything in Shona, our native language. For example, the words for "I swear like that." is *Nda pika so.*

As I walked around I observed that there was one young man who was painting the backgrounds to the canvasses and placing them on newspapers spread on the ground in the shadow of

Valentine and I drove to his house which was a few blocks on the other side of the road. Getting to his house, it felt like I was driving in a labyrinth of narrow roads, alley ways and sanitary lanes all crisscrossing each other in a tiny densely packed typical Harare township housing setting. I could only drive my car into the labyrinth up to a point but not to his house because the only access to the house is a footpath. I left the car in the alley way and followed Valentine to his house.

We found Valentine's mother working in the yard. She greeted me heartily. She was just as open and charming as her son. She recognized me through my family name as the son of Harare's then famous photographer. Like most African mothers I grew up under, she immediately wanted me to come and sit down and have tea in her home. The charm and grace she showered me with the invitation into her home belied the obvious humble meager existence of her family and their abode. The family, living, dining and most probably by night someone's bedroom, room was bare but clean, dominated by the large sofa that had seen better days and I could tell that the television set sitting on a small table standing against the wall, did not work because it was serving as a base for cups and pots. This was not very different from the other homes in similar neighborhoods I had been in. All the same, I sat down and enjoyed the first of many visits that I have made to that house.

Valentine lifted and turned a stretched canvas that was on the floor leaning against the wall in the room. I could not tell what it was because it was still a sketchy work in progress. I asked him what it was and he told me it was an abstract painting which he expected to complete in a few days. I could barely contain my excitement because I felt and shared in his confidence that it was going to be something special.

I thanked them for their hospitality and promised to come back in a week.

A week later I drove back into the neighborhood to follow up and see what Valentine had done with the work in progress. When I drove in, my memory could only take me up to the place where I had left the car the previous week.

I could not remember how to get to Valentine's house. So, I asked one of the kids who were playing in the dirt.

"Do you know where Valentine's house is?" my question was met with curious but blank stares.

"You know Valentine? The artist who draws pictures?"

Their faces lit up and one of them shouted,

"You mean PICASSO?"

Hearing the name "Picasso" a second time in that wretched distressed neighborhood floored me and drove me to uncontrollable stitches of laughter as I followed the children running ahead leading the way to Valentine's house..